Studies in Sociology

Edited by

PROFESSOR W. M. WILLIAMS

University College, Swansea

I

THE SOCIOLOGY OF INDUSTRY

STUDIES IN SOCIOLOGY
Edited by Professor W. M. Williams

THE SOCIOLOGY
OF INDUSTRY

S. R. PARKER
Office of Population Censuses and Surveys

R. K. BROWN
University of Durham

J. CHILD
University of Aston in Birmingham

M. A. SMITH
University of Salford

SECOND EDITION

London
GEORGE ALLEN & UNWIN LTD
RUSKIN HOUSE · MUSEUM STREET

FIRST PUBLISHED IN 1967
SECOND IMPRESSION 1968
THIRD IMPRESSION 1969
FOURTH IMPRESSION 1970
FIFTH IMPRESSION 1971
REVISED EDITION 1972
SECOND IMPRESSION 1975

Cloth Edition ISBN 0 04 300033 9
Paper Edition ISBN 0 04 300034 7

PRINTED IN GREAT BRITAIN
in 10 on 11 point Plantin
BY COX & WYMAN LTD
LONDON, FAKENHAM AND READING

CONTENTS

Note :
The names against chapter titles indicate who was responsible for preparing the first drafts. All four authors took part subsequently in the process of revision and of integrating the chapters according to an agreed framework. However, the views expressed in each chapter remain the responsibility of its original author.

INTRODUCTION TO SECOND EDITION

During the four years since the first edition of this volume appeared, a substantial amount of new material on the subject of industrial and occupational sociology has been published. In order to provide an up-to-date account of developments in this field, we have completely revised the original text, deleting some (but by no means all) older references to make room for newer ones. Although the structure of the book as a whole is basically unchanged, we have taken this opportunity to attempt to remedy the defects of the earlier edition, notably the too cursory treatment of some topics. We also aim in this edition to present a more balanced account of the role of theory in the sociology of industry, and to avoid giving the false impression that structural–functional theory has a monopoly in this field.

This book is addressed mainly to students of sociology who are especially interested in its application to the 'world of work'. It is intended as an introduction, but assumes that the reader is not completely unfamiliar with the sociological approach to the study of society. The purpose of this book is twofold: to synthesize the growing body of relevant empirical material, and to show how sociological theory at different levels of analysis treats the three interrelated aspects of the subject matter. It is these three inter-related aspects that constitute the three sections of the book.

The first section is at the social system level of analysis, and examines the relation between industry and other sub-systems or institutions of society. We discuss specifically education, the family and stratification as sub-systems each of which affects industry and is affected by it. At this level, industrial sociology forms part of a wider economic sociology, which is the application of the general frame of reference, variables and explanatory models of sociology to the complex of activities concerned with production, distribution, exchange and consumption.[1] However, the purely economic aspects of these activities, which form the subject matter of theoretical and applied economics, are outside the scope of this book.

The second part of the book, constituting the second level of analysis, is concerned with the internal structure of industry and the roles that individuals play in that structure. Organization theory is the link between analysis of systems and of work

[1] N. J. Smelser, *The Sociology of Economic Life* (Englewood Cliffs: Prentice-Hall, 1963), p. 32.

organizations. We attempt, therefore, to analyse organizational structures and processes, giving particular attention to authority and technology as aspects of work organizations. These aspects include informal organization, technology and technical change, the structure of management, and some key problems in industrial relations between management and unions.

Roles also feature in the third part of the book, but here, instead of being linked to the structure of organizations, they are seen as the actions and pre-disposition to action of individuals and of groups. This part is concerned with the relation between work and non-work behaviour and attitudes, and it corresponds roughly to what is sometimes defined as the sociology of occupations. It includes an analysis of some of the main features of the labour force, adjustments to work roles by occupational groups, and the interaction between work and non-work life.

There are, of course, different approaches to the whole subject matter of sociology and long-standing but still active debates about the validity of competing theories of society. We intend neither to ignore these differences nor to write exclusively from one or other standpoint. To some extent the threefold division of our book parallels three phases in one of the central debates in sociology: that between 'systems' theorists and 'action' theorists. To oversimplify the positions of these theorists, they represent respectively the view that 'society makes man' (systems), and 'man makes society' (action).[2] Part I of our book may be seen primarily as an exercise in systems analysis, and Part III as an exercise in action analysis. Part II stands at the intersection of system and action, requiring both perspectives to be brought into the picture, and in this sense it is the pivotal part of the book. We believe that in the study of organizations there is a need to use, if not combine, both a systems and an action approach. This means seeing the structure and functioning of organizations partly as systems of social relations and partly as the consequences of motivated action by groups and individuals.

We have distinguished the subject matter of a broadly defined industrial sociology at three theoretical levels with two further considerations in mind. First, the theoretical framework must be congruent with a sociological perspective applicable to other fields of analysis. Secondly, existing empirical and theoretical contributions to the field of industrial sociology require a logical form permitting consistent analysis of levels of contribution and identification of levels, as well as types, of problems. This second

[2] D. Silverman, *The Theory of Organisations* (Heinemann, 1970), p. 40.

consideration may lead us sometimes to point out that research is lacking or inadequate in some areas. Also, relating a large amount of material to a theoretical framework can over-simplify the complexity of the phenomena; it should not be implied that the development of sociological theory is more advanced than in fact it is. Our treatment of theory is not intended to put empirical research into a straitjacket; rather, we view theory as a guide to the planning of research, the results of which in turn can serve to modify theory.

No one who sets out to write a book on sociology organized around a theoretical framework succeeds entirely in relating all his material to that framework, and we are no exceptions. Although we have tried to include some consideration of what seem to us to be the more important research findings and theories, inevitably in a book of this small size and large scope the treatment of each topic is brief. The interested reader will, however, be able to follow up particular topics through the references given and the suggested further reading.

CHAPTER 1

What is Industrial Sociology?

INDUSTRIAL sociology is an important and fascinating subject. Its importance is clear; industrial pressures and processes, and the world of work, play a central part in shaping the kind of society in which we live and the kinds of choices we make about life styles and priorities. The way society is organized and the way we live are inextricably bound up with the network of institutions and roles we call industrial society. This too is the fascination of the subject. For in asking 'what is industrial sociology?' we are really asking about the kind of society in which we live. Is it a society dominated by conflict in which there tends to be a continuous struggle between individuals and groups for control over resources, both social and economic? Or is it rather a society held together by shared values and interests which are generally recognized and important? Is it a society best viewed as a network of institutions which dominate and shape people's lives? Or is it rather that people have interests and aims which pattern the basic institutional framework? These questions and their answers are fundamental to an understanding of industrial society and to a large extent underpin much of the analysis in the book.

Yet the importance and fascination of industrial sociology extend further than these initial questions. Industrial society is a particular kind of society. It is one in which science is increasingly applied to resolve basic problems of human organization and need. It is rational in that it is characterized by institutions and organizations which are specialized in their structure and function. It is rational too in the sense of giving people access to and control over the social world and, fundamentally, control over their own choices and relationships. It is a society which has turned upon itself the enquiring and organizing ethos of science and seeks to explain the patterning of its own social organization and objectives.

Sociology has an important part to play in this process. It is an attempt by man to explore his social world. Sociology acts as a catalyst of change; it points to the consequences of particular policies and shows just how effective they are. It provides data which sometimes only confirm people's experience, but more often reveal basic knowledge about how society works. It is concerned with provision and planning and with the conflicts over access to and use of different kinds of resources. Sociology is an agent of change and in this role justifies a focus upon 'industrial sociology'. Industrial structures and processes, especially technology, have increasingly a direct influence on the fabric of society and the quality of people's social relationships. We intend to examine these structures and processes in detail and explain the consequences they have for people in different areas of life.

To say that sociology shares with science a stress on the rational appraisal of its subject matter and a curiosity about how it persists and changes is perhaps only half the story. They also share a common methodology based on the belief that by quantifying phenomena and testing propositions it is possible to say something meaningful and useful about the world. This is a reasonable belief, but not one which goes unchallenged when the methods of science, such as classification and measurement, are applied to human behaviour and social relationships. Behaviour itself is continuous rather than discrete and tends to flow over from one situation to another. It is not easily divisible into isolated units. Situations are themselves not always a good guide to understanding why people behave in particular ways. People's motives and aims may not be directly related to the situation they are in. Individuals themselves possess some awareness of the consequences of their own behaviour and they can change the analysis and predictions made about them. They are not the relatively passive and un-self-reflective phenomena of the natural sciences. Since people can attach meaning to their own actions it is equally problematic to establish how people interpret their own behaviour. The sociologist may regard it as fitting into one category or model whilst the individual himself may define it in quite a different way. These are fundamental issues in the social sciences which should not be ignored, even though sociology and the natural sciences may lay claim to the same methodology.

To some extent these fundamental issues find expression in the way this book is organized. It is in three sections. The first section is an *institutional approach* which views society as a system or network of interacting institutions. The concern is to link together the general features of the economy with the family, education and other sub-systems of society. At this level of abstraction very broad generalizations can be made and propositions about the way structures are patterned can be established. This is a complex analysis which embraces both historical and functional elements of institutional structures. Industrial sociology, then, in the first part of the book is an examination of such structures and the processes which link them.

The second section of the book focuses at a lower level of abstraction on the factors which influence the structures and processes of organizations, particularly work organizations. Organizations gain some depth by being viewed comparatively, and so the characteristics of the firm are seen in the wider context of features general to all organizations. The goals pursued, the kinds of technology, communication and authority systems which exist and the nature of organizational conflict, are the main concerns. Industrial sociology in this part of the book is an examination of the structure of organizations and the factors which shape their external and internal relationships, such relationships themselves being grouped around the roles people occupy and the production systems with which they interact.

Most people do not see the world in terms of institutions or organizations. They view the world through their own behaviour and relationships, at the interpersonal level. As has been suggested, the way people view their own behaviour and the meaning they attribute to social relationships are fundamental sociological issues. The third section of the book attempts to explore from this perspective the meaning of work and the ways in which people relate themselves to their occupations.

From the foregoing discussion we can say something about the aims and content of industrial sociology. It is an examination of industrial structures and processes from an institutional-systems perspective; from an organization-role perspective; from a role-person perspective. These are different levels of analysis and involve different theoretical claims. Broadly the institutional-systems perspective embodies what is known as the structural-functionalist approach, while the role-person perspective owes its pedigree more to the social action framework of explanation. The use of these two theoretical approaches should be reasonably familiar to the reader who has some knowledge of sociology. In a crude way they parallel the distinction in economics between macro and micro analysis. In the sense that organizational analysis provides a bridge between 'systems' and 'action' the middle section of the book is a pivotal one, containing some discussion of functionalist theory and the interactionist approach.

Classical social theorists

Since the intention is to draw together a wide range of material it is important to see how other writers have approached the subject of industrial sociology. One major approach has been through the classical theorists of sociology, notably the works of Marx, Weber and Durkheim. Each had a distinct view of industrial society and of the way in which the economic system is organized.

For *Marx* the important focus was ownership of the means of production. Economic classes were seen to be formed on the basis of property ownership, the bourgeoisie were the exploiters and the proletariat the exploited. These two classes were in perpetual conflict and their relationship determined the broader social framework of society. Religion and culture—in fact all social phenomena—were believed to be a direct outcome of the dialectical struggle which would culminate in the classless society. Workers under capitalism were alienated and only the dissolution of the property basis of society would free them from the tyranny of capitalism. Marx's analysis projected both exploitation and alienation for the proletariat, to be changed only through revolution.

Weber extended this analysis by maintaining that interest groups existed on bases other than property ownership. Life styles and culture were not, he thought, directly tied to property. Weber's focus was slightly different too from that of Marx, in that his interest was in the uniqueness of capitalism rather than how far it typified the history of all societies. For Weber industrial society was unique because it was characterized by substantive and functional rationality—by the growth of rationality as a thought system via the growth of science, and the growth of rational organizational forms. Bureaucracy typified this latter emphasis on rational and routinized structures. Disenchantment and the loss of personal freedom were the consequences Weber feared could result from the major structural and cultural trends of industrialism.

Durkheim too saw dangers, but of a different kind. The basic forces for change he located in 'division of labour', the process by which activities and obligations became more specific and specialized, particularly in the economic sphere. Industrial society possessed a high division of labour and this had a direct consequence for the network of social relationships and social norms which provided the framework for people's behaviour. Choice became a conscious process, and as societies increase in volume (number of people) and density (frequency of interactions) the sources of consensus became important. The legal and moral framework and a variety of reference groups, for Durkheim, were such sources. He saw the danger of societal disorganization, the process of anomie, which had as its consequence the breakdown of the legal and moral order and the detachment of people from their reference groups. People in this process could lose any real sense of belonging. Anomie was an abnormal form of the division of labour and industrial society could pose the problem of societal disintegration in its most acute form.

The classical social theorists provided important leads into the significant questions and areas of analysis in industrial society. They certainly pointed to the overwhelming importance of industrial structures and processes in shaping all levels of society. They also shared a concern for the impact of such structures and processes on the societal mechanisms of conflict and consensus. How economic and social interests are regulated and reconciled, and the nature of the groups through which they are expressed, were prominent questions for Marx, Weber and Durkheim, and they are for us. Such interests and interest groupings usually operate within some kind of organizational structure, whether it be the firm or some broader economic or societal setting. This structure itself was an important focus for the classical theorists. Of special import for industrial sociology was Weber's model of bureaucracy—more generally the nature of authority and communication systems in industrial organizations and particular work settings. This traditional concern has also found expression at various points in our text. These concerns have not been treated equally in the development of industrial sociology but they have been well established as focal questions for analysis.

Contemporary formulations

The broad areas of contemporary studies in industrial sociology are well outlined by Tom Burns:[1]
(1) Bureaucratization and its impact on professional and black-coated workers.
(2) The workplace as a complex organic or socio-technical system.
(3) Studies of work groups (mainly informal) and their contrast with management.
(4) Analysis of the 'industrial relations' complex—the nature of conflict and bargaining procedures and the growth of trade unions.
(5) A general concern with the impact of industrialization on the individual.

[1] T. Burns, 'The Sociology of Industry', in A. T. Welford (ed.), *Society : Problems and Methods of Study* (Routledge, 1962).

These five areas certainly reflect very different interests and their diversity owes something to the problem-oriented approach which has characterized post-war industrial sociology, particularly when used as an adjunct of management theory. There has been no attempt to relate these areas to a broad framework of explanation or to integrate the findings in each field. Fortunately this situation is changing and giving way to a conceptually and empirically integrated body of findings. The key to such an integration is a broadening and deepening of the field of enquiry. J. H. Smith defines it rather generally as 'the study of social relations in industrial and organizational settings, and of the way these relations influence and are influenced by relations in the wider community'.[2] Lupton has been more specific and advanced 'the study of the social system of the factory and of the influences external to the factory which affect that system'.[3] Etzioni has made a claim for the subject to be an extension of organization theory.[4] Nosow and Form make out a special case for occupational sociology based upon five major themes: the study of individual occupations; the study of the occupational structure; the relationship of both to general aspects of the social structure; the link between work and social phenomena such as leisure, retirement, unemployment; and finally the usefulness of a particular occupation to throw into relief a social problem.[5]

None of these various definitions is of itself sufficient to embrace the total framework for industrial sociology. The general perspective and insights from sociology need to be applied to a particular area and that area needs to contribute its own insights and data. Some mention should be made of Schneider's analysis which fits in well with this approach.[6] He suggests that there are certain parallels between sociology in general and industrial sociology. For example the informal group in industry is a counterpart to the clique or gang found in the wider society. Industrial organizations are only one kind of organization and share common characteristics with others, such as coercive and voluntary organizations. Conflict is not limited to industrial contexts and may occur at various points in the social fabric. Types of social action may be recognized in the industrial setting but may be

[2] The University Teaching of the Social Sciences: Industrial Sociology (UNESCO, 1961), p. 31.
[3] Ibid.
[4] A. Etzioni, A Comparative Analysis of Complex Organizations (New York: Free Press, 1961).
[5] S. Nosow and W. H. Form, Man, Work and Society (New York: Basic Books, 1962).
[6] E. V. Schneider, Industrial Sociology (New York: McGraw-Hill, 1969).

found in all kinds of situations. We would not dispute Schneider's view that sociology is a specializing and generalizing science. Indeed such a view is implicit in the wide scope of this book and the stress on different levels of analysis.

Quantitative and qualitative analysis

Some suggestions have already been made about the difficulties of a scientific approach to human behaviour. These difficulties relate not only to the framework of explanation but also to the ways in which the predicted links in the framework are tested. The purpose of methodology is to establish the existence of such links and their degree of generality. This is made difficult by the variability and complexity of human behaviour although it may not, in principle, be impossible. Certainly the attempt should be made. Sociology relies upon quantitative and qualitative assessment to embrace the scope of its subject matter, its richness and diversity.

Quantitative analysis and techniques are varied and it is only possible to consider here a few of the basic assumptions and claims made, particularly in the use of statistical approaches to the analysis of behaviour. Random sampling is the basis of most probability predictions made in statistical analysis. This simply means that all factors under consideration have an equal chance of being selected—there is no attempt to bias the initial selection of subject matter to be analysed. Random selection ensures that the results obtained from samples can be used to make statements about whole groups or 'populations'. It makes possible a high level of generalization and reveals general patterns of behaviour to be found in such groups. Like all analysis—and all of science—the statistical results of the process can be said to apply 'at a given level of probability'. They are not unconditionally true for all occasions.

Statistics has its basis in quantification, in being able to give a numerical value to whatever is being analysed. This is not too difficult for many aspects of behaviour. For example, the number of married women who work and the contribution this makes to the income of the typical family can be fairly easily assessed. But other kinds of behaviour are less easy to quantify. The enjoyment of a piece of music, the love and companionship which two people share, the feeling of how good it is to be alive—these are much less amenable to description and analysis by statistical techniques. There is perhaps no reason why they should be—we could all fill in questionnaires which ask us to decide what 'good to be alive' consists of, and the general features of 'music we enjoy'.

But this still would not capture the vitality and depth of the experience and the influence it may have on us. Statistical analysis has its limits. It makes possible statements about general features of groups or selected populations, but in the process may lose the depth and richness and variety of the data itself. And if the requirement of randomness is lost or impaired then quantification takes on the spurious guise of truth.

Qualitative analysis is an attempt to encompass the diversity and complexity of human behaviour and social relationships. The purposive nature of human choice, and the framework of meaning within which human action occurs, impose certain difficulties when an attempt is made to move beyond a simple behaviourist or data collection approach to social explanation. The aim of Weber, 'the interpretative understanding of social action so as to arrive at a causal explanation of its course and effects', is a desirable one. The difficulty is that it means linking observations about the meaning of behaviour with sets of norms—or expectations—and with sets of symbols, which themselves may be experientially or culturally discrete.[7] People may not share the same framework of meaning. Situations too can be very complex and possess an 'emergent' quality which makes them difficult to analyse and predict.

One solution adopted by sociologists is that of participant observation. This is the process of participating in a situation or relationship so as to observe and understand its meaning. The method has several merits; the observer can immerse himself in the situation to grasp its subtlety and complexity—the variations in the 'framework of meaning' can be explored rather than lost in the desire to make generalizations about typical cases. The observer can assess the less quantifiable aspects and relate them to the rich and varied patterns of social interaction. Participant observation, then, is useful but has some disadvantages. Generalization is sacrificed to detail—there is no justification for the observer to make claims beyond the immediate situation except in the most tentative terms. Coupled with this is the difficulty of quantifying the detail he does observe. It seldom falls into convenient categories. The observer too can influence the situation —he can introduce bias and create a situation which differs somewhat from what may have existed had he not been present. The ability to generalize and the reliability of the method are the basic weaknesses of participant observation. However, even with these

[7] For a fuller discussion see Chapter 7; also D. Silverman, *The Theory of Organizations* (Heinemann, 1970).

reservations, it does form an important part of sociological enquiry.

Not all sociologists, however, can enter into every situation and evaluate the subtleties and nuances. Qualitative assessment is therefore also part of the development of 'sociological imagination' or theory building. Theories—and hypotheses of which theories consist—derive to some extent from the marriage of quantitative analysis and participant observation. With the results of statistical techniques and participant observation in relation to any one problem, it may be possible to develop a theory which explains why certain relationships exist and how they change with different circumstances. Certain links may be clear from the data, for example that different kinds of work produce different kinds of satisfaction and rewards, or that work which allows very little freedom to the individual creates intense dissatisfaction or alienation which colours his whole view of work and may spill over into other areas of life. To note this relationship is one thing, but to fit it into a model which links different kinds of work technologies to different family and work attitudes is quite another. It means using imaginative insight and drawing-out from the data all kinds of implications and links. These can be tested later, but the process of fitting them together to form a working model is a process akin to theorizing in the natural sciences.[8]

Conclusion

Industrial sociology is important because industrial structures and processes shape every aspect of human life and are deeply embedded in the social fabric of societal and personal choices. To understand, predict and control those pressures and processes is a fundamental objective; it is the probing and shaping by man himself of the kind of society he wants and considers worth striving for. In this process all social knowledge is valuable, whether it is quantitative or qualitative, and sociological awareness becomes part of the critical assessment of the choices to be made by man in relation to his social context.

[8] See particularly B. G. Glaser and A. L. Strauss, *The Discovery of Grounded Theory* (Weidenfeld and Nicolson, 1968).

CHAPTER 2

The Economy:
Structure and Change

AT the outset it is necessary to say something about the scope of economic and sociological analysis and the extent to which they overlap. Economics has consisted of the intensive study of one type of function in, or sub-system of, society: that of producing, distributing and exchanging goods and services. This has also been the subject matter of one branch of sociology, namely economic sociology, but in a way less specific to economics and more general to social institutions. The motives of individuals and groups and the nature of social processes are the concern of sociology; it is the specific effects of these motives and processes on the production and use of different goods and services that fall within the scope of economics.

The conception of the economy as a sub-system of society implies a wider conception of society as itself constituting a system. We shall deal in Chapter 7 with the general features of the 'social systems approach' to the study of society, but here it should be noted that it is possible to view the economy as the parent system which itself consists of a number of component parts or sub-systems. Each of these component parts may further be seen as bearing the same functional relation to the economic system as this bears to the social system as a whole. Thus Parsons and Smelser have suggested that the economy has adaptive, goal-achieving, integrative and pattern-maintaining (latency) functions, represented respectively by the capitalization and investment sub-system, the production sub-system (including distribution and sales), the organizational sub-system or entrepreneurial function, and economic commitments such as physical, cultural and motivational resources.[1] A more concrete structure, such as a market

[1] T. Parsons and N. J. Smelser, *Economy and Society* (Routledge, 1956), Chapter II. See also N. J. Smelser, *The Sociology of Economic Life* (Englewood Cliffs, N.J.: Prentice-Hall, 1963), especially Chapter 4, for a more general sociological analysis of economic processes.

or a firm, may also be analysed in a similar way. Ingenious though such theoretical analyses of economic organization and behaviour may be, it is doubtful whether they can take us very far in understanding similarities and differences in real situations. Perhaps their chief value is in enabling us to map out the whole area of sociological interest at the societal level.

In examining the economic sub-system the matter is complicated by the fact that whereas, for example, the family as a sub-system of British society has no significant functional relationship with the family system of other countries, the British economic system is part of a world economy which has evolved a complex network of institutions serving to regulate the relationships and activities of its various parts.

Over the last century the position of the British economy has declined vis-à-vis other industrialized countries and—as measured by gross national product—has fallen from first to sixth place among the world's economies.[2] It is this secular decline which provides a broad economic context indispensable to any meaningful analysis of the economic and social policies of British governments and policy-makers in the post-war years. Successive balance of payments crises culminating in two devaluations of the pound may, from this standpoint, be seen as reflecting a relative decline in the international competitiveness of the British economy. Thus many of the issues and problems relevant to the study of the sociology of industry (reorganization and redundancy in the textile and ship-building industries, for example) may be understood not only as problems of adjustment at an individual or group level but also as a function of economic problems at a system level.

Below we shall deal briefly with some of the more specific changes that have taken place in recent decades in the economic sub-system in Britain. In subsequent chapters in this part of the book we shall examine the interrelation of the economy with other sub-systems of society.

CHANGES IN THE ECONOMIC STRUCTURE

In an exploratory study of the sociology of the economy some middle course must be steered between a static view of the economy as it is today and a long historical view going back at least to the beginning of the Industrial Revolution. For purposes of empirical research it is often unavoidable to take a static view of some feature

[2] *Main Economic Indicators* (OECD, June 1971).

of economic behaviour or structure, but the researcher must be wary of generalizing his findings to other times and places in which they might not hold good. Thus although most economists treat both employment opportunities and supply of labour offered as mainly functions of price, where social prestige factors make leisure preferable to work price changes may have a negligible influence on labour supply.[3] But strictly speaking the view of the economic structure over time is primarily the province of the economic historian and the view over space (beyond modern industrial societies) the central focus of the social anthropologist. Accordingly, we shall concentrate on an analysis of some of the main present features of, and trends of change in, the economic structure in twentieth-century Britain.

Technology

Our first theme under the general heading of technology is the growing importance of industrial as against agricultural activities. In 1851 agriculture and fisheries accounted for 22% of the occupied population in Britain; the proportion fell to 8% in 1911, 5% in 1951, and is now about 3%.[4] The development of industry has been accompanied by widespread changes in our whole way of life: the growth of towns, cities and conurbations, of transport and communication systems, and of consumer goods which have reduced household drudgery and extended the scope, albeit the mechanical nature, of leisure-time activities.

New inventions, technological advances and shifts in world demand have altered radically the character of British industry in recent years. Industries in which new techniques have predominated, notably electronics, aircraft, motor and chemicals industries, new branches of machinery construction, and petroleum are contributing a significantly larger share of the total output and of total exports and providing wider employment opportunities for an increasingly skilled labour force. We shall return to this theme when discussing the influence of technology on the social structure in industry (Chapter 9) and the changing occupational structure (Chapter 12).

Our second theme concerns the increasing application of technological methods in industry. Expenditure on industrial and scientific research has increased steadily, and facilities for technical education have been greatly enlarged. But the existence of inventive genius and organized research is only one factor in

[3] S. Rottenberg, 'Income and Leisure in an Underdeveloped Economy', *Journal of Political Economy*, April 1952, p. 101.
[4] Cf. G. C. Allen, *The Structure of Industry in Britain* (Longman, 1970).

what Florence calls the self-perpetuating 'circular' character of the train of causation.[5] Certain material, product and market conditions are necessary for inventive genius or organized research to have affected production. Although it is often said that we are entering an atomic age, technology has not moved forward evenly over industry as a whole.[6] Automated factories already exist in such industries as chemicals and engineering, but the construction industry is closer to the craft age (though prefabricated factory building is on the increase).

Values

Values play an important role in providing the rationale for particular norms or rules of organization or conduct. Appropriate values are equally necessary with material conditions to enable a certain kind of economic and social system to be developed and to operate. In modern industrial societies a very high value has been assigned to economic productivity. The need to maximize profits or wages and the need to work hard reflect values peculiar to our own and closely related societies; such values are found only rarely in other parts of the world.[7] Even within the context of advanced industrial societies profit maximization, long held to be the main, if not the only, goal of economic enterprise, has come to be questioned. Thus Galbraith has suggested that the 'technostructure' (the name for all who participate in group decision-making or the organization which they form) is compelled to put prevention of loss ahead of maximum return.[8] Autonomy (the ability to set prices, organize product demand, ensure supplies, and so on), and the taking of business not for its profit but 'to hold the organization together' are values which are coming increasingly to surpass those of profit maximization.

Notwithstanding the crudity of such analogies as 'Great Britain Ltd', the pursuit of economic growth has been the equivalent at the societal level of profit maximization at the level of the industrial organization. But even growth is coming to be questioned as a terminal value. The view has been cogently argued by Mishan that the continued pursuit of economic growth by Western societies is more likely on balance to reduce rather than increase social welfare.[9] He further suggests that we should reject economic

[5] P. S. Florence, *Economics and Sociology of Industry* (Watts, 1969), p. 10.
[6] D. C. Miller, 'Influence of Technology on Industry', in F. R. Allen *et al.* (eds.), *Technology and Social Change* (New York: Appleton–Century–Crofts, 1957), p. 266.
[7] E. V. Schneider, *Industrial Sociology* (New York: McGraw-Hill, 1969), p. 16.
[8] J. K. Galbraith, *The New Industrial State* (Penguin, 1969), Chapter 10.
[9] E. J. Mishan, *The Costs of Economic Growth* (Penguin Books, 1969), pp. 219, 223.

growth as a prior aim of policy in favour of a policy of seeking to apply more selective criteria of welfare to re-create an environment that will gratify and inspire men. Although this view is at present a minority one, it serves to emphasize that values are problematic and that what we have come to think of as 'conventional wisdom' concerning economic means and ends may be ephemeral.

Values differ from society to society, and *within* societies there may be different prevailing values in each. The sub-cultures of management and labour are different enough for these two groups to possess somewhat different values toward each other's roles, sometimes to the extent of conceiving their own to be basic to the productive process and that of the other group to be expendable or even parasitic. But inconsistent general values may be contained within the same society, provided that they are 'rendered compatible by their distribution among various statuses in the social structure so that they do not result in conflicting demands upon the same persons at the same time.'[10]

Organization

During the past hundred years or so the British economy, in common with those of other advanced industrial societies, has shown an expansion in industrial output and an increase in imports; the economy has become increasingly differentiated and specialized as a manufacturing unit. The process of differentiation of goods produced and services offered has also been accompanied by the localizing of particular industries.[11]

Part of the process of development of the economy is the trend towards increasing size of industrial factories or plants. Between 1955 and 1961 the proportion of people employed in establishments with eleven to twenty-four employees fell from 3·6% to 2·7% (no reliable figures are available for establishments employing ten or fewer persons).[12] The majority of business enterprises, however, remain small; of the 55,000 manufacturing establishments in 1961, at least 40,000 employed fewer than 100 people, while only 1,200 employed 1,000 or more people.[13] The size of units is limited in some industries by the conditions of production and in others by the character of demand. Thus in building repair work and in much road haulage the output is

---

[10] R. K. Merton, *Social Theory and Social Structure* (Glencoe: Free Press), 1957, p. 502.
[11] For details see Florence, *op. cit.*, especially Chapter 3.
[12] *Annual Abstract of Statistics*, 1956, p. 124 and 1969, p. 132.
[13] *Ibid.*, 1969.

scattered and erratic, while in other industries small-scale operations occur where firms make types of product for which demand is limited.[14]

Another trend in industry is the growing proportion of organizers, managers, and research, technical and administrative staff compared to actual working operatives. The ratio of staff to operatives in British manufacturing industry has risen from 11·8% in 1924 to 30·2% in 1964.[15] American evidence is that staff has increased less than the rise in productivity level. This probably holds good for Britain and is a consequence of increased output due to the use of machines which displace the operative but add to the work of staff. This trend towards higher staff ratios is likely to continue with the increasing application of science to industry and greater forward planning, budgeting, and other management procedures.

One important consequence of the increasing size of industrial organizations is the trend to monopoly or oligopoly. Supporters of capitalism have long been in a contradictory position on monopolies: they are seen as having economic advantages resulting from larger markets, can enable production to be rationalized, but are also 'in restraint of trade'. Despite legislation against them, they still flourish in Britain and America. The latest monopoly technique—the takeover—has become the subject of much concern and some enquiry. Although statistics over time are sparse, it has been estimated that approximately 10% of the United Kingdom's total non-nationalized assets changed ownership in 1967-8, and that 70% of the top 100 largest firms were bidding or were taken over in the two years.[16] Another estimate is that in the four years 1967-70 perhaps one-fifth of all assets of industrial and commercial companies was acquired by other companies.[17] An Acton Society Trust study of takeover bids and mergers found that they often occurred in declining industries faced with a falling demand for their products (sometimes accompanied by diversification of activities) and between companies where horizontal or vertical integration could bring economies of scale.[18] One consequence of takeovers is to concentrate ownership and control even further; also they often have

[14] D. Burn (ed.), *The Structure of British Industry: A Symposium*, vol. II (Cambridge University Press, 1958), p. 441.

[15] Florence, *op. cit.*, p. 16.

[16] G. D. Newbould, *Management and Merger Activities* (Guthstead, 1970), p. 198.

[17] A. Glyn and B. Sutcliffe, 'The Critical Condition of British Capital', *New Left Review*, March–April 1971.

[18] E. Goodman, *The Impact of Size* (Acton Society Trust, 1969), pp. 54–5.

the unfortunate effect of losing people their jobs through redundancy.

A question to ask when considering the structure of the economy is: who owns the wealth of the country? It is sometimes asserted that increasing taxation has narrowed the gap between the property owners and the propertyless, but the facts do not bear this out. In 1968 the wealthiest 10% of the population aged fifteen or over owned 75% of the wealth,[19] a proportion that has not changed markedly since pre-war years. However, income is more evenly distributed: out of a total of nearly 28 million incomes in 1966, there were only about 58,000 of more than £5,000 a year after tax.[20] The changes in distribution of income that have taken place as a result of increased and differential taxation are difficult to measure, but clearly those with very high gross incomes now retain proportionately less than they did pre-war.

The organization of industry and its effect on the economy as a whole, particularly in regard to labour matters, has been much influenced in post-war years by the growing power and authority of workers organized in trade unions. During the war trade unionists sat with employers' representatives on joint production committees in many industries, and the Trades Union Congress was called upon to play an important part in the formulation of economic policy. The gradual relaxation of wartime controls over labour and industrial relations and post-war full employment put the trade unions in a far stronger position than ever before. Trade union leaders were appointed to the boards and commissions responsible for industries brought under public ownership, and union membership has risen to its present figure of ten million. Trade unions have grown into large, national, relatively tightly organized bodies. Industry has become more complex and concentrated, and the parts of the economy more interdependent, thus giving union action wider repercussions.

The social consequences of full employment

For much of the post-war period the unemployment rate varied between 1% and 2% of the employed population—a situation conventionally described, with some justification, as full employment, since a majority of those affected were either temporarily stopped or unemployed for not more than eight weeks. Towards the end of the 1960s, however, the unemployment rate began to rise, and by late 1971 had reached 4%. But taking the post-war period as a whole in comparison with the 1930s, it has been one of

[19] *Hansard*, October 27, 1970, vol. 805, col. 26.
[20] *The British Economy* (Central Office of Information, 1969).

full or at least near-full employment. The social consequences of this are relevant to a study of the structure and change of the economy.

An expanding economy and the stronger market position of workers vis-à-vis employers has led to 'affluence' of the working class, at least relative to the poverty of many of its members before the war. Two developments have aided the expansion of the consumer market in post-war years: the growth of advertising and of hire-purchase sales. It has been estimated that in 1970 approximately £800 million was spent on all forms of advertising in Britain, or about 2% of the total national income. The expansion of the teenage market for consumer goods and services, especially for clothes, records and other products of the 'leisure' industries, is a direct result of the favourable market situation of most juvenile workers, with employers clamouring for their services and hence pushing up wage and salary rates.[21] Although a circular process of demand and supply of labour and commodities is involved, the consumer is by no means the key factor in the situation. Rather, it is the producer who as a rule initiates economic change, and consumers are educated by him if necessary; they are, as it were, brought to want new things.

The rapid growth of sales of household and durable consumer goods has been greatly helped in recent years by instalment purchasing. Despite fluctuations caused by intermittent government regulation of the terms of hire-purchase and credit sales agreements in order to help boost or damp down the economy, the total hire-purchase debt outstanding shows a strong upward trend. From about £490 million in 1958 it rose to about £1,400 million in 1971 (some of this increase is due to inflation). The need to keep up, and if possible expand, demand for consumer goods has led to 'planned obsolescence' of products built not to last but to be replaced by later models more frequently than is really necessary. Obligations to repay hire-purchase debts have been said partly to account for an increasing tendency on the part of many workers to choose paid overtime rather than more leisure when basic working weeks are reduced.

Another consequence of full employment—labour mobility—will be dealt with in Chapter 12 from the point of view of the individual, but its relation to the needs of the economy may be briefly mentioned here. The main movement of population in recent years has been towards the South-East and the Midlands and away from Scotland, Wales and North-West England. These

[21] K. Roberts, *Leisure* (Longman, 1970), p. 46.

changes reflect the rise and decline of industries: the contraction of coal-mining, shipbuilding and the textile industries, and the growth of the metal, vehicle, aircraft, electrical and similar industries. Hunter and his colleagues have analysed the economic consequences of technological change with particular reference to three industries—printing, steel and chemicals. They point out that adjustment to technological change and resulting problems of industrial relations are only one way in which the growth of state interest and intervention in labour market policy is exemplified.[22] As we shall see in Chapter 11, developments in industrial relations policy and practices—which are not unrelated to the state of the economy and views on what to do about it— are perhaps taking place more rapidly than developments in any other sphere in which industrial sociologists are interested.

[22] L. C. Hunter et al., Labour Problems of Technological Change (Allen & Unwin, 1970), p. 355.

CHAPTER 3

Industry and Education

THE relations between industry and education are reciprocal, and have consequences for the structure of both institutions. On the one hand, there are the demands of industry for trained workers, or for those sufficiently well educated to be suitable for appropriate training; on the other hand, industry itself has an educational 'sub-system', including apprenticeship and on-the-job training schemes of various kinds. For the individual there is the half-way stage between being a student and being a worker that is implicit in the provision by some employers of day-release and 'sandwich courses'. At the individual level there is also the question of occupational choice and transition from school to work, a process that may involve problems of role and status in a changed social and physical environment.

THE INFLUENCE OF INDUSTRY ON EDUCATION

One of the most obvious ways in which the world of work affects the world of learning is in the choice of subjects in schools and the ways in which these are taught. What is often called the vocational bias in education means that education is regarded as a direct preparation for a particular kind of occupation. Employers want a convenient method of sorting out suitable applicants for jobs; a paper qualification obtained by examination is one such method, and hence the school curriculum often tends to be treated simply as a means to examination success.

Several types of school have a vocational bias, in a direct or indirect sense. Technical schools, which are attended by only about 6% of the secondary level pupils in Britain, are designed to afford entry to skilled manual and some non-manual occupations. Secondary modern schools, which are attended by about three-quarters of children between eleven and fifteen, often have vocational courses that can sometimes be a greater source of interest than purely academic subjects, but in recent years there has been a move towards education for non-work life. Among secondary modern schools in Sheffield, Carter found that although some courses had a vocational bias the children were not conditioned to specific types of work, but their interests and aptitudes were encouraged in the light of opportunities of local employment.[1]

The 1944 Education Act, which legislated for secondary education for all, has formed the basis of subsequent educational policy. Three types of secondary school—modern, grammar and technical—were provided for, 'differentiated in terms of their curricula, but equal in prestige'. However, while it has been possible to achieve some degree of parity of conditions, the essential corollary 'parity of esteem' has been more elusive. As Banks remarks, 'in so far as the grammar school selects an able minority of children and prepares them for middle-class occupations it is still fulfilling an elite function and representing an elite philosophy of secondary education'.[2] The trend towards greater occupational rewards for educational qualifications has brought the educational system into closer relation with the occupational structure.

Those who accept that the school has legitimate functions in preparing children for vocational life point to a number of advantages that this may have. It may reduce the opposition of parents (and of children themselves) to extended schooling if this is seen as a means of getting a better-paid job. It may help to make the school syllabus more interesting and relevant to everyday life. And it may help to reduce the problems associated with the transition from school to work. These and a number of other advantages that are claimed for the school as a means of vocational preparation are discussed by Thomas.[3]

Criticisms of the vocational bias in education have centred around a concern that the links between education and industry may be at the expense of the role of education in other spheres of life. Thus Bantock writes that 'one's feeling about the Crowther Report [on education between fifteen and eighteen] is that the needs of the practical life and of vocationalism have taken up their abode unashamedly and that it is the element of humanization which has been forced into a corner of the living-room, though

[1] M. P. Carter, *Home, School and Work* (Oxford: Pergamon Press, 1962), p. 11.
[2] O. Banks, *The Sociology of Education* (Batsford, 1968), pp. 23–4.
[3] L. G. Thomas, *The Occupational Structure and Education* (Englewood Cliffs: Prentice-Hall, 1956), pp. 446–62.

the need to recognize its presence there has not been forgotten'.[4] There were similar reactions to the Robbins Report on higher education. Mannheim and Stewart expressed their concern with the narrowness of vocational education thus: 'although it produces the necessary cogs and wheels in the social machine, specialist education disintegrates both the personality and the mental powers for understanding the human situation which has to be mastered'.[5] None of these criticisms affects the fact that the needs of the occupational world inevitably impinge on the educational world, though the extent to which this happens in different types of society may be the subject of comparative study.[6] The difference of opinion arises from value judgments, and centres on the relative weight that should be given to vocational and non-vocational education.

Technical education

In the nineteenth century industry as a whole was apathetic and even hostile to technical education. The inferior prestige of science, and particularly technological studies, has acted as a brake on both the expansion of provision in science and technology and the attraction of students to such courses.[7] The low status of the scientist in industry was the result chiefly of the pre-eminence in the nineteenth century of mainly non-scientific industries and the perpetuation of the neglect of scientific instruction by recruitment and promotion policies. A major factor accounting for industry's lack of support for technical education has been the small proportion of technically qualified men in higher management. Clark concluded from his survey in 1956 that more managers held non-technical than technical qualifications, though he added the remark that 'the common picture of a graduate from Oxford and Cambridge, with a degree in the arts, dominating management does not appear to be true for present-day industry'.[8]

Several factors have contributed to the post-war expansion in technical education. Successive economic crises and foreign competition in export markets have underlined the importance of the application of scientific methods to production, especially in the newer industries such as chemicals and electronics.

[4] G. H. Bantock, *Education in an Industrial Society* (Faber, 1963), p. 114.
[5] K. Mannheim and W. Stewart, *An Introduction to the Sociology of Education* (Routledge, 1962), p. 161.
[6] H. Hans, *Comparative Education* (Routledge, 1961), p. 64.
[7] S. Cotgrove, *Technical Education and Social Change* (Allen and Unwin, 1958), p. 190.
[8] D. G. Clark, *The Industrial Manager* (Business Publications, 1966).

Government-sponsored research organizations have played a part by demonstrating the practical value of research. The increase in the scale of industrial organizations has enabled the largest of them to undertake more research and training of personnel in various branches of science and technology. Employers' associations, though not teaching bodies, have in some cases concerned themselves closely with the development of education and training for management, including the technical side.

Technical education is extremely heterogeneous and is carried on in a variety of educational establishments. Apart from secondary technical schools, there are technical colleges, technical institutes, colleges of further education, schools of art and craft, and so on. In recent years a number of colleges of advanced technology have been established which run courses of a standard comparable with that of university degree courses and these are mostly now designated as or have become universities. There are also more recent qualifications, such as the CNAA degrees. Technical colleges are organized in four tiers according to the nature of their work. Below the colleges of advanced technology, regional colleges do much similar work but also less advanced studies; below these, area colleges do mostly technician and craft work; and, at the bottom, the local colleges do only this low level work.[9]

One controversial question concerns how much technical training should be provided by firms and how much by outside educational bodies. Specific training for a single job peculiar to the work and processes of the firm is usually regarded as the responsibility of the firm. But it is argued that more general education and training can and should be given outside the firm. To a large extent, size of firm determines whether technical education or training can be provided. In large firms work-based training schemes are feasible, but smaller firms without the necessary manpower and facilities are forced to rely on externally-based arrangements. With technical training provided by firms there is also the problem of one firm 'poaching' the labour that another has had the expense of training.

The spread of automation is likely to have important effects both on technical training in particular and on education in general. Because of the complexity and abstractness of the new industrial techniques, a theoretical university education will increasingly tend to carry more weight than apprenticeship and 'on-the-job' training. One consequence of this is to make promotion from the shop floor more and more difficult and to reduce occupational

[9] A. Beveridge, *Apprenticeship Now* (Chapman and Hall, 1963), p. 114.

and hence intra-generational social mobility. Working foremen, with no more technical training than those they supervise, will tend to be replaced by better qualified people, perhaps graduates who spend a short period at the first level of supervision as a preparation for a higher management post.[10]

THE INFLUENCE OF EDUCATION ON INDUSTRY

Educational and training courses that take place wholly or partly within the firm reflect to some extent the purposes and values that are attached to education in the wider society. Such courses, including the system of apprenticeship, together with the effect of a better-educated labour force on the composition and distribution of manpower resources, constitute the chief influences of education on the industrial world.

Apprenticeship

The system of apprenticeship has changed little since the Middle Ages when, as a paternalistic relationship between the craftsman and the trainee, it formed an integral part of the guild system. Today the paternalism has largely vanished, but many of the associated customs remain. Apprenticeships are served, mostly for periods of four or five years, from the ages of fifteen or sixteen. During that period the youth has a mixture of on-the-job and back-to-school training, for which there are no universal standards laid down and no terminal tests or examinations of competence required. Some employers train their apprentices well, while others do not. Some firms impose stringent intelligence and adaptability tests, while others take on a few lads because they have always had apprentices around the workshop. Although the 1965 Industrial Training Act provides for imposing training levies on entire industries (thereby making it less profitable for firms to 'buy' apprentices with higher wages as they emerge from training), there is no legal obligation on any employer to provide training. Small wonder that the apprenticeship system has been described by one critic as 'that makeshift, class-ridden, inadequate, anachronistic contract which perpetuates master-servant relationships and the confusion, if not the exploitation, of the young in a sphere which cries out for enlightened and flexible forms of occupational training for *all* young people'.[11]

[10] There is a great difference between industries in the proportion of qualified people employed. In clothing and footwear only 0·71% had higher educational qualifications, compared with 37·67% in professional and scientific services, Central Statistical Office, *Qualified Manpower in Great Britain* (HMSO, 1971), p. 42.

[11] P. Paterson, 'The Apprenticeship Scandal', *New Statesman*, January 14, 1966.

An enquiry by Williams revealed that apprentices were rarely, if ever, actually *taught* their trade.[12] The system relies on skilled men to teach them, and many are not good teachers. Williams, among others, advocates admission to the ranks of skilled workers as a result of a test of competence instead of the passage of time. Another problem is that although apprentices theoretically emerge as skilled craftsmen much of the work they are put to would be regarded objectively as semi-skilled, because of the fragmentation of many industrial processes. Since the great need of industry is for semi-skilled technicians, the apprenticeship system encourages unrealistic and rigid job definitions.

A survey of apprentice technicians in a Home Counties technical college found that their biggest grumble was lack of opportunity to use their abilities.[13] Forty per cent thought they did not receive enough instruction at work, and nearly as many were dissatisfied with the instruction given. This was particularly so among those coming from small firms where facilities for instruction were likely to be poorer. The survey also tested attitude differences among the three types of apprentice—Ordinary National Certificate, Technical, and Craft, which represent levels of educational performance ranked in that order. The Craft apprentices were significantly less aware than the others that they had unused abilities, and attached less importance to promotion prospects. These findings support the thesis that levels of occupational aspiration and expected achievement are conditioned by educational attainment and subsequent type of course attended, involving its own style of socialization for work (see below).

Day-release and sandwich courses

Off-the-job training, including the academic side of apprenticeship, consists of such arrangements as day-release to technical colleges and sandwich courses. Both serve the function of filling in the gaps that most on-the-job training leaves. Day-release means that young workers are given time off from work—usually one day a week—to attend courses of study at technical colleges of various types. There are three main levels, leading to professional, technician and skilled craftsman occupations.[14] The purpose of the course largely determines its length, varying from three to five years at the technician and skilled craftsman level up to seven years or more for professional qualifications. The

---

[12] G. Williams, *Recruitment to Skilled Trades* (Routledge, 1957), p. 194.
[13] T. S. Chivers and S. R. Parker, 'The Apprentice Technician and his Job', *Industrial Society*, October 1966.
[14] P. F. R. Venables, *Technical Education* (Bell, 1956), p. 112.

professional courses usually include one or two evenings or Saturday morning attendance each week.

Day-release is generally assumed to be a privilege conferred on young employees—usually apprentices—at the discretion of their employer. But engineering craft apprentices in federated firms have the *right* to day-release for technical training up to eighteen—normally one day a week, payment to be made at the *time rate* of wages. Release from engineering, shipbuilding and electrical goods industries accounts for more than a third of all release. Industries which give relatively little day-release are generally either those which require little training of their workers or which provide on-the-job training.

Venables discusses the reasons for the different degrees of support given to day-release by various industries. Where a high standard of technical skill and knowledge has been necessary to the survival of the industry, this motive has been powerful enough to compel educational progress. In such trades as service and distribution, however, the benefits to the employer are less tangible. Not only is working time lost, but the knowledge that many a competitor does not give release and that when the period of training is finished the youth may be attracted elsewhere are strong deterrents to day-release.

Sandwich courses are so called because 'layers' of full-time college study and industrial experience alternate over a period of years, for example, six months in industry succeeding six months in college for three or four years. Sandwich courses present many administrative difficulties on both the industrial and educational side and have been slow to develop. In 1959 it was estimated that there were fewer than 8,000 students on such courses in England and Wales.[15] As compared with day-release, sandwich courses give much better opportunities for integrating academic study with industrial practice, which is especially important in training for management. A study by Cotgrove and Fuller suggests that the influence of sandwich courses on occupational socialization and choice is minimal.[16] However, the strength of these courses may be the extent to which they provide a more relevant educational experience, and contribute to motivation and achievement and to the maturation of the student.

Manpower and education

Up to World War I there were three main groups in industry,

[15] P. F. R. Venables, *Sandwich Courses* (Parrish, 1959), p. 20.
[16] S. Cotgrove and M. Fuller, 'Occupational Socialisation and Choice: the Effects of Sandwich Courses', *Sociology*, January 1972.

corresponding to various phases of technical development
unskilled manual, skilled manual, and commercial and clerica
personnel. In recent years machines have taken over much clerica
work and the unskilled manual occupations now contain a
relatively smaller proportion of the labour force.[17] The distinction
between manual and non-manual, which rests on the older and
somewhat false distinction between workers 'by hand or by brain'
is becoming blurred. We are moving towards having a labour
force containing a broad stratum of semi-skilled workers doing
varied work, and trained technical employees. Accordingly, it
is claimed that vocational training for the mass of workers will
have to be increasingly on the model of the semi-skilled technician.[18] Abstract and 'human relations' qualities will be more
often required to organize and supervise the work.

The increasing displacement and occupational mobility of
labour brought about by the introduction of new machines and
techniques has special consequences for the education of employees. To invest too heavily in a specialism may give a man
capabilities that are so specific to one job that he is unable to
undertake another job without retraining.[19] There is a great need
for retraining of displaced workers; in 1970, 12,600 people passed
through the 52 Government Training Centres, but this represented
only a fraction of the potential candidates for training.

Another link between industry and education is the tendency
for large companies to encourage their senior employees to send
their children to public schools. Some firms (such as Shell)
have established insurance schemes to help pay school fees.[20]
Others provide closed scholarships for employees' children. Still
others make substantial contributions to the finances of public
schools. Not only are private firms helping to subsidize the public
schools, but they are also encouraging the science side to be
developed. Industry has also given similar help to universities,
with the emphasis less on social status and more on technical and
managerial education.

SCHOOL AND WORK

Although, according to the plan of this book, the role-person

[17] G. Friedmann, *The Anatomy of Work* (Heinemann, 1961), p. 176.
[18] H. Schelsky, 'Technical Change and Educational Consequences', in A. H.
Halsey *et al.*, *Education, Economy and Society* (Glencoe: Free Press, 1961).
[19] P. W. Musgrave, *The Economic Structure* (Longman, 1969), p. 43.
[20] E. A. Johns, *The Social Structure of Modern Britain* (Oxford: Pergamon Press,
1965), p. 111.

level of analysis of the relation between industry and education should be deferred to Part Three, it seems more appropriate to deal with it here. The transition from school to work may be considered under two headings: the aspirations and expectations that school leavers have concerning the occupational world, and the process of occupational choice.

Aspirations and expectations

Schoolchildren form certain impressions of the occupational world from different sources. At school they pick up bits of information about various occupations, though this information may be a little more direct when the syllabus includes such subjects as current affairs or social studies. The family is often an important source of information (and sometimes misinformation) about jobs and of instilling, in varying degrees or not at all, a motivation for achievement.[21] Also, the mass media of communication may impart direct information given by people interested in vocational guidance and may also convey impressions and stereotypes of occupational roles as portrayed in films and on television.[22]

Various studies have been concerned with how schoolchildren and young workers view aspects of the occupational world. A survey by Musgrove of boys and girls aged fourteen to twenty in a northern industrial region showed that work was instrumental for them, but for other than crudely material ends; it was referred to largely as a learning situation (in a broad sense) by both manual and non-manual employees.[23] Hill's study of boys in fourteen maintained grammar schools in the Midlands indicated that among the section who had not made up their minds on the choice of a career (56% of the total) the overwhelming majority were more interested in conditions of work and material rewards.[24] Maizels concluded from her survey of children in the London suburb of Willesden that there is a general lack of correspondence between the needs and expectations of young people on the one hand, and what is provided by the relevant community services, including industry, on the other.[25] Vocational aspirations were

[21] D. C. McClelland *et al.*, *Talent and Society* (New York: Van Nostrand, 1958), and subsequent articles.
[22] M. L. DeFleur, 'Occupational Roles as Portrayed on Television', *Public Opinion Quarterly*, Spring 1964, who claims these portrayals are 'selective, unreal, stereotyped and misleading'.
[23] F. Musgrove, *The Family, Education and Society* (Routledge, 1966), p. 108.
[24] G. B. Hill, 'Choice of Career by Grammar School Boys', *Occupational Psychology*, October 1965, p. 286.
[25] E. J. Maizels, *Adolescent Needs and the Transition from School to Work* (Athlone Press, 1970), p. 303.

higher, on average, than were subsequent achievements. There was, overall, a reduction in the average level of skill, training, and education required in the jobs actually obtained compared with those originally preferred.

The extent to which juvenile expectations of work are realized must often have a profound effect on the individual. As Keene points out, the work environment influences the development of the young person as a citizen.[26] The example of fellow workers and supervisors may be as important as that of parents. In this respect the 'work experience' schemes run by some schools are of interest.[27] Selected groups of senior children visit factories and offices to gain practical knowledge of the world of work. The criterion of suitability of employers is that they really should provide their visitors with a job to do, but should not regard them as a potential source of full-time employees. Such schemes are on a smaller and less centrally organized scale in Britain than in countries such as Sweden.

Theories of occupational choice

There has been a good deal of attention paid in recent years to the process by which young people come to choose a particular occupation. Earlier theories were developed in America by Ginzberg, Blau and their associates.[28] In this review we shall concentrate on more recent British work in this field.

Musgrave has put forward a conceptual framework as a first approach to a theory of occupational choice.[29] The central focus of this is the process of socialization, which is seen strictly as learning to take roles: 'Anticipatory socialization is important. At each stage of socialization roles may be rehearsed in such a way that transition to the next stage is more easily accomplished.' By getting to know role prescriptions associated with particular occupations, the young person is said to be able to choose an occupation that more or less matches his wishes from among the limited range available to him.

Coulson and her associates have criticized Musgrave's approach as an 'attempt to explain social behaviour in terms of an over-

---

[26] N. B. Keene, *The Employment of Young Workers* (Batsford, 1969), p. 183.

[27] M. Clemans, 'School–Work–School', *Trends in Education*, July 1969.

[28] E. Ginzberg *et al.*, *Occupational Choice: An Approach to a General Theory* (New York: Columbia University Press, 1951); P. M. Blau *et al.*, 'Occupational Choice: A Conceptual Framework', *Industrial and Labour Relations Review*, 9, 1956.

[29] P. W. Musgrave, 'A Sociological Theory of Occupational Choice', *Sociological Review*, March 1967. A useful collection of *Sociological Review* papers (including two by Musgrave) is W. M. Williams (ed.), *Occupational Choice* (Allen & Unwin, 1974).

simplified functionalist theory which rests on a consensus model of society'.[30] By ignoring the significance of variation and conflict, Musgrave is able to define the 'significant others' of the new employee as 'managers and work-mates', without considering that their demands may be very different. He also implies a value orientation towards a static social order, in which only unusual people change their jobs or work alone. Ford and Box make a more fundamental criticism of the use of the term 'choice' in connection with first employment: 'Surely, one might argue, the transition from school to work in most cases [of boys and girls leaving school at fifteen] cannot be described as *choice* at all? These children do not know the full range of jobs open to them and have no efficient criteria for differentiating one job from another.'[31]

Two of the best-known theories of the entry into employment are those of Ginzberg and Super. Both stress that we need to consider the entry into employment as a process. But whereas Ginzberg attaches prime importance to the individual's growing awareness of his own interests and capacities, Super places greater stress upon the role of the individual's social environment in structuring the individual's conception of his interests, abilities and capacities. Roberts believes that both theories are inadequate to explain the differences he found among his sample of young men interviewed about their jobs and ambitions: he suggests instead that the momentum and direction of school leavers' careers are derived from the way in which their job opportunities become cumulatively structured and young people are placed in varying degrees of social proximity, with different ease of access to different types of employment.[32]. The ambitions of school leavers adapt to the directions that their careers take, and are not major determinants of the occupations that young people enter.

[30] M. A. Coulson et al., 'Towards a Sociological Theory of Occupational Choice —A Critique, Sociological Review, November 1967.

[31] J. Ford and S. Box, 'Sociological Theory and Occupational Choice', Sociological Review, November 1967.

[32] K. Roberts, 'The Entry into Employment', Sociological Review, July 1968.

CHAPTER 4

Industry and
the Family

THE interaction between industry and the family is on two levels:
relations between industrial organization and family structure as
sub-systems of society and, on the role-person level, relations
between the occupational and familial life-spheres of individuals.
We first consider the influences that types of modern industrial
organization have on the pattern of family life and the way in
which occupational roles influence family roles. We then enquire
to what extent family patterns exert pressures on various forms of
industrial organization and behaviour, and how the individual's
commitment to family life influences his performance in his job.
Various types of relationship between work and family spheres
of life are examined. Finally, we consider the special question of
the increase in the proportion of married women who go out to
work and the social prerequisites and consequences of this
increase.

THE INFLUENCE OF INDUSTRY ON THE FAMILY

The influence of industry on family life may take direct and
indirect forms. In the direct form, the circumstances and attitudes
associated with a certain kind of occupation affect circumstances
and attitudes in the family sphere. In the indirect form, the
association between occupation and family is mediated through
social class membership, that is, being in a given occupation is
associated with being in a certain social class whose members, in
turn, show characteristic behaviour patterns and attitudes. There
is no rigid distinction between occupational influences and
social-class influences, and much of the empirical study of the
relation between occupation and other spheres of social life rests

upon 'social-class' data.[1] However, in considering the influence of industry on the various aspects of family life the extent to which social class may also be a factor should be borne in mind.

Husband-wife roles

Industry, directly or indirectly, helps to shape the roles that are played within the family, as well as the relationship between these roles. In general, family and work spheres have become increasingly differentiated, due mainly to the specialization of work roles in industrial society.[2] However, when we look more closely at the degree of integration of work and family life at various socio-economic levels we see particular differences.

The role of the husband in the upper-class family may have little relationship to his role at work, and there may be little carry-over of the prestige and authority gained at work into family life. Work commitments tend to minimize the amount of time and energy that the husband can devote to his family, which becomes a subordinate part of his life. In the middle class, the financial standing and status of the family is more dependent on the occupation of the husband. But to the extent that he follows a technically complicated occupation that is incomprehensible to his family, his wife cannot identify strongly with his work. However, the working-class husband's occupation gives neither high income nor status in society at large. In communities where it is traditional for the husband only to work, the separation of occupational and family life is almost complete. In working-class families where the wife also goes out to work, the additional income is often used to make the home a more comfortable place to stay in, and the husband's family role may be more like that of the middle-class husband.

From their research Blood and Wolfe characterized the main role of the wife in relation to her husband's occupation as collaborative, supportive or peripheral.[3] Farm wives much more often than urban wives collaborated with their husband's jobs. The wives of white-collar workers most often thought they helped their husbands by giving encouragement, considerateness or entertainment (supportive), while the wives of blue-collar workers either contributed only housework or nothing (peripheral). The mixed effects of company policy on the family life of mobile

---

[1] Cf. S. Nosow, 'Social Correlates of Occupational Membership', in S. Nosow and W. H. Form (eds.), *Man, Work and Society* (New York: Basic Books, 1962).

[2] R. and R. Rapoport, 'Work and Family in Contemporary Society', *American Sociological Review*, June 1965.

[3] R. O. Blood and D. M. Wolfe, *Husbands and Wives* (Glencoe: Free Press, 1960), p. 91.

executives have been noted by Bennis and Slater.[4] By trying to include the wife and family in their thinking, many large corporations have acted alternately to stabilize and to rupture the marital bond; the former through including the family in corporation activities, providing therapeutic facilities, and so on; the latter by demanding that the husband's organizational commitment always come first, and by penalizing the husband for the wife's personality and behaviour.

Another influence of work factors on husband-wife roles is seen in the various ways in which husbands can seek to reconcile the demands of work and family life. Concentrating on studies of middle-class 'spiralists' (those with progressive careers and residential mobility), Edgell links success at work and family life in the following ways:[5]

TABLE I

Orientation to success at work	Central life interest(s)	Roles	Family life relationships
high	work	segregated	husband-dominated
medium	home and work	role conflict	inconsistent
low	home	joint	egalitarian

The three rows represent three possible solutions to the problem of conflicting influences, one in favour of work, one in favour of home and a third in favour of both or neither. The spiralist who is 'married' to his work and successful in it is (like the 'upper-level' husband discussed above) likely to segregate his work role from that of his wife in the home and (more doubtfully) to exercise a dominating influence in the home. The husband who is unsuccessful in his work may compensate by making home his central life interest, sharing family roles and influence with his wife. But the husband oriented to success in both work and family roles may experience conflict between them and fluctuate in his attachment and relationships. As with much theory, this approach to a typology of work and family roles and relationships is developed from existing research results and needs to be tested and possibly modified by research designed for that purpose.

[4] W. G. Bennis and P. E. Slater, The Temporary Society (New York: Harper, 1968), p. 90.
[5] S. Edgell, 'Spiralists: Their Careers and Family Lives', British Journal of Sociology, September 1970.

Kin relationships

The network of relationships with members of the extended family shows the influence of occupation, both directly and indirectly. Bott's intensive study of a small number of English urban families suggests that ties among kin are likely to be stronger if they are able to help one another occupationally. In class terms, families with close-knit networks are likely to be working-class, but not all working-class families have close-knit networks.[6] The strength of the family's neighbourhood network depends more directly on the husband's occupation within a given class. If he is engaged in an occupation in which his colleagues are also his neighbours, his network will tend to be localized. If he is in an occupation in which his colleagues are not his neighbours, his network will tend to become loose-knit.

Millward has examined a further aspect of the interaction between kin relationships and work behaviour: that of the different arrangements by which mainly working-class young women contribute to family income between leaving school and getting married.[7] He distinguishes two main types of arrangement: 'giving in' means that the girl hands in her wage-packet to her mother and receives pocket-money; 'on board' is when the girl gives her mother an agreed sum for board and lodging and keeps the rest for herself. Although the process of 'going on board' is to be seen as an essentially domestic matter, it appears that on any occasion when the girl's earnings are substantially raised the subject is likely to come up in family discussion. Millward and his colleagues used the domestic arrangements by which workers contribute to family income to help explain changes in family life and behaviour at work.

Socialization

The father's experiences in the world of work are transmitted to the child both directly via occupation and indirectly via social class position. For some occupations the home may be the office or shop, and the family will be aware of many of the father's job activities.[8] In some families the father will be very uncommunicative about his work, while in others the father may communicate

[6] E. Bott, *Family and Social Network* (Tavistock, 1971); see also C. R. Bell, *Middle Class Families* (Routledge, 1968).

[7] N. Millward, 'Family Status and Behaviour at Work', *Sociological Review*, July 1968.

[8] W. G. Dyer, 'The Interlocking of Work and Family Social Systems Among Lower Occupational Families', *Social Forces*, May 1956.

virtually every detail of his work to his family. This is partly a matter of the types of personality involved, but is also related to the 'visibility' of the father's occupational role and the extent to which work is an integral part of life. Thus in farming households it is easy for children to start doing jobs around the farm without conceiving of these as 'work', and quite likely that they will also become farmers because the range of alternative occupations appears more restricted than to urban dwellers. By contrast, the technically complex and therefore less visible occupational role of many middle-class urban fathers means that they cannot serve as role models for their children.

The class position of the father has important influences on the socialization of the child.[9] At each level of society there tends to be a typical role pattern for children. Among upper-class families the care and raising of the child is often left in the hands of others besides the parents. The socialization of the child is directed at transmitting to him the values and norms of the upper classes. By contrast, middle-class children and parents spend much more time together. Socialization in the middle class aims to teach the child to behave 'properly', and more depends on the child's ability to compete successfully with others for the best education and hence for the best jobs. But working-class children are rarely driven to succeed or to live up to high standards of propriety; the emphasis is on obedience and keeping out of trouble.

Studies have been made seeking to test the influence of types of occupation on the severity or otherwise of socialization techniques. Research in Detroit reported by Miller and Swanson attempted to relate methods of child-rearing to the type of father's occupation.[10] Occupations were divided into those that demand initiative, individual action and risk taking (entrepreneurial) and those emphasizing conformity to established practices and the decisions of superiors (bureaucratic). The authors' hypothesis was that certain types of occupation attract certain types of husbands and wives and in turn create philosophies that are reflected in family behaviour. The hypothesis was borne out by results: 'entrepreneurial' parents were more likely to train their children in self-control at an earlier age and in a greater number of respects than were 'bureaucratic' parents.

A further enquiry by McKinley considered the variables of autonomy, power and satisfaction in the work situation (within

[9] E. V. Schneider, *Industrial Sociology* (New York: McGraw-Hill, 1969), pp. 499–502.
[10] D. R. Miller and G. E. Swanson, *The Changing American Parent* (New York: Wiley, 1958).

social class) in relation to socialization.[11] He found that more fathers in jobs low in autonomy used severe socialization techniques than did those in high autonomy positions. The same applied to those with no subordinates in the work situation compared with those with subordinates, and to those dissatisfied with their work compared with those satisfied. But the author warned against overlooking the problem of what kinds of personalities choose different types of occupation, and stressed that more thorough study is needed before any conclusion can be made about causal processes.

THE INFLUENCE OF THE FAMILY ON INDUSTRY

Most available evidence points to the greater influence of industry on the family than vice versa, but it must not be supposed that family patterns and values have a negligible influence on industrialism or occupational life. As an example of the importance of family structure in facilitating or hindering social change, Goode has compared the efforts of Japan and China to industrialize during the late nineteenth and early twentieth centuries.[12] Starting with similar social and economic conditions, Japan became far more industrially advanced than China during the early part of the twentieth century. Family differences between the two countries contributed to the differences in the rate of industrialization in several ways: the inheritance system in Japan made it easier to accumulate wealth for investment, nepotism was less a handicap than in China, and those who rose socially did not need to help the undeserving members of their families.

The present Japanese industrial system, despite being as technically advanced as that in many Western societies, provides an example of what Form and Miller call a 'family-mediated' type of industry–community relations.[13] The Japanese factory tends to be family-like in the roles and norms of its employees; employment is normally for life, there is emphasis on intragroup harmony rather than on individual competition, and paternalistic care of the employee, even in his private life.[14] A similar pattern

[11] D. G. McKinley, *Social Class and Family Life* (New York: Free Press, 1964), Chapter 7.
[12] W. J. Goode, *The Family* (Englewood Cliffs: Prentice-Hall, 1964), pp. 114–16.
[13] W. H. Form and D. C. Miller, *Industry, Labor and Community* (New York: Harper, 1960), p. 394f.
[14] J. C. Abegglen, *The Japanese Factory* (Glencoe: Free Press, 1958); K. Odaka, 'Traditionalism, Democracy in Japanese Industry', *Industrial Relations*, October 1963.

may be seen in those Western industrial organizations where family values are dominant, often associated with family ownership of the enterprise or with religious or co-operative communities.

Family life is of concern to employers because a well-adjusted family member tends to be regular and punctual, better satisfied in his job, and a good team-worker.[15] Trade unions also generally approve a family system that produces loyal members, and this is especially so in certain craft unions where the 'union ticket' is still often passed from father to son. A person's home life may affect his job performance, and in large organizations there is sometimes a psychological consultant to smooth out home problems that may interfere with an employee's ability to work well.

From his study of familial and occupational roles in America, Salvo found that an engineer's willingness to accept a better position and his extent of involvement in community affairs are related to the stage of family life cycle.[16] However, family cycle does not appear to be related to involvement in professional activities. Salvo concluded that 'the values and aspirations of individuals are less influenced by massive readjustments in institutional relationships than was previously thought, and that the exigencies of situational and positional features associated with familial roles remain significant in this technological society'.

Types of work–family relation

We have seen that, at the institution-system level of analysis, the relation between industry and the family may vary between subordinating family life to the needs of industry to mediating purely industrial values with family values. To the extent that the structure and functioning of industrial organizations have a reciprocal relationship with the family life of employees, the analysis is also theoretically straightforward. At the role-person level, however, we need to look more closely at the factors influencing work and family interrelation and to develop a theoretical framework into which research findings may be fitted, so far as possible.

As a starting point we may take one of the postulates of the Rapoports: work and family roles tend to be isomorphic (affecting

[15] D. C. Miller and W. H. Form, *Industrial Sociology* (New York: Harper, 1964), p. 599.
[16] V. J. Salvo, 'Familial and Occupational Roles in a Technological Society', in R. Perrucci and J. Gerstl (eds.), *The Engineers and the Social System* (New York: Wiley, 1969).

each other in such a way as to induce *similar* structural patterns in both spheres) or heteromorphic (inducing different structural patterns).[17] Of the studies and observations that have been cited so far in this chapter, the family in which the wife collaborates with her husband in his work, the family whose home is attached to the father's office or shop, the farming family, and to some extent the modern Japanese family, all exhibit isomorphism of work and family life, or an extension of one sphere into the other. The other studies may be analysed into two further groups. If isomorphism represents a *positive* relationship between spheres, there is a *minimal* (approaching nil) relationship, as well as a *negative* relationship between them. A minimal relationship between work and family spheres is exemplified in families in which the husband's occupational role does not impinge on his family beyond affording it a certain style of life. Unlike the positive or negative patterns, the husband's occupational role has low visibility to his family. Occupations with regular hours, with no marked physical or psychological effects on the holder, and that do not encroach on free time, are cases in point. Another way of putting this is to say that, in the life pattern as a whole, the relationship between work and family for these people is neutral rather than one of extension or opposition of spheres.

Having considered the patterns of extension and neutrality of life spheres, we are left with the pattern of opposition. This pattern is seen typically in those manual occupations that generate in the husband a need for family life to function as compensation. Thus to repair the damage exacted by his work the miner tends to expect his wife to feed and comfort him, making few demands in return.[18]

These three patterns of relationship between work and family spheres—extension, neutrality and opposition—are theoretically applicable to the relationship between other life spheres. We shall return to this question in Chapter 14 when discussing the relationship between work and leisure. Meanwhile some of the features of these patterns, so far as work and family life are concerned, may be discerned. They are summarized in the table.

The conclusions of some further research on work and family patterns may be fitted into this typology. A study by Podell showed that those who tended to be specific (orienting to others as means) or affectively neutral in their occupational role-expectations were more likely to view their occupational and

[17] R. and R. Rapoport, *op. cit.*
[18] N. Dennis *et al.*, *Coal is Our Life* (Eyre and Spottiswoode, 1969).

TABLE 2

Type of relationship between spheres	Extension (positive)	Neutrality (minimal)	Opposition (negative)
type of occupation	farming, small shopkeeper, certain professional or craft	technical, routine non-manual	mining, fishing some 'impersonal' occupations
occupational characteristics	home and work location (partly) co-extensive	low visibility of occupation to family	physically or psychologically damaging work
husband's familial role in relation to occupational role	continuous with work	alternative to work	recuperation from work
role of wife in relation to husband's occupation	collaborative	supportive	peripheral

familial lives as distinct and separate.[19] Those who were occupationally diffuse (responding to others as 'total persons') and
effective were more prone to want their family included in their
vocational world. These correspond to the neutrality and extension
patterns respectively. The study by Aberle and Naegele of
middle-class fathers' occupational roles points to the element of
opposition between work and family behaviour that exists for
those in some business occupations.[20] The business world limits
responsibility and authority, judges people by what they can do
rather than by who they are, and often makes aggressiveness pay
off—the opposite of which generally applies to successful family
life.

Another example of opposition of spheres was revealed in the
investigation by Dynes, who found that unsatisfactory interpersonal relationships in the family were significantly related to
high occupational aspiration and satisfactory family relationships

[19] L. Podell, 'Sex and Role Conflict', *Journal of Marriage and the Family*, May
1966.
[20] D. F. Aberle and K. D. Naegele, 'Middle-Class Fathers' Occupational Role
and Attitudes Toward Children', in N. W. Bell and E. F. Vogel (eds.), *A Modern
Introduction to the Family* (Routledge, 1961).

to low occupational aspiration.[21] However, this probably reflects a culturally-based psychological need to succeed in at least one life sphere rather than a relationship between occupational and family life variables. Finally, research showing the extent to which members of certain occupations have their central life interest in the family sphere helps to test the hypothesis that impersonal occupations tend to lead to a higher affective investment in the family, and personal occupations to a lower investment in the family. Among a sample of bank employees, 35% gave family-oriented responses to a group of questions on central life interest, among youth employment officers 25%, and among child care officers 19%—and these occupations are on a scale of decreasing impersonality.[22]

MARRIED WOMEN WORKING

Women constitute one-third of the labour force in Britain, and of these nearly two-thirds are married. Census figures show that the proportion of all married women gainfully employed has risen steeply over the last few decades—it was 9% in 1921, 21% in 1951, 32% in 1961, and 41% in 1970. About half of them work part time.[23] The age group that has had the greatest increase is the 35–44 years. The children of these women have usually reached school age, thus affording the mothers more spare time in which to take up a job.

Conditions making increase possible

The factors making an increase in the employment of married women possible may be considered under three heads: opportunity, capacity, and motivation. Concerning *opportunity* there have been five main factors, the first three in relation to the industrial structure as a whole, the other two being more specific to particular industries:

(1) *Shortage of labour.* During the last war it was necessary to recruit women to fill jobs left vacant by men in the forces, and many women stayed on in employment after the war. The manpower shortage was aggravated by a longer education and training period for juveniles and an increasing proportion of dependent old

[21] R. R. Dynes et al., 'Levels of Occupational Aspiration', *American Sociological Review*, April 1956.
[22] S. R. Parker, unpublished further analysis of a study reported in *The Future of Work and Leisure* (MacGibbon and Kee, 1971), Chapter 7.
[23] A. Hunt, *A Survey of Women's Employment* (HMSO, 1968), p. 25.

people to working population. Firms have been encouraged to establish branches in isolated areas to make use of possible reserves of married women.

(2) *Changes in the occupational structure.* Increased expenditure on consumer goods has led to an expansion in the retail trade, which employs large numbers of women. Welfare and administrative workers for the social services, whose numbers have grown, are mainly women.[24]

(3) *Social disapproval weakened.* The presence of increasing numbers of single women in industry, greater equality in marriage, and the emancipation of women generally, have resulted in the breaking down of traditions about a woman's place being in the home. However, these traditions persist in certain areas, for example, mining communities.

(4) *Discrimination removed.* For example, the ban on married women teachers was lifted in 1944 and on married women in the metropolitan police force in 1946.

(5) *Changes in industry.* To encourage the employment of married women some factories have introduced special shifts allowing time for married women to do their domestic duties. 'Controlled absence' has been accepted by some employers.[25] With the introduction of new machines, manual work has become lighter and more amenable to women.

With regard to *capacity*, the health of the average working-class housewife has been improved with the benefits of the welfare state. The middle-class housewife has generally had no experience of primary poverty that saps vitality and initiative. Labour-saving devices, by reducing the amount of work required to run the home, have helped to increase the capacity for outside employment.

The *motivation* for married women to work has been the subject of several investigations.[26] The great majority of married women stress that they have financial reasons for working, though in most cases this is to secure a higher standard of living generally or certain specific extras, such as children's education, rather than economic necessity. The desire to escape boredom and loneliness at home and to gain companionship at work has been shown to be an important additional motive, while for some, but relatively few working-class wives, the job itself is intrinsically interesting.

[24] V. Klein, *Britain's Married Women Workers* (Routledge, 1965), pp. 14–17.
[25] R. K. Brown et al., 'The Employment of Married Women and the Supervisory Role', *British Journal of Industrial Relations*, March 1964.
[26] V. Klein, *op. cit.*, pp. 36–44; R. K. Brown et al., *op. cit.*; P. Jephcott et al., *Married Women Working* (Allen and Unwin, 1962), pp. 87–8, 99–111.

Status striving is sometimes a motive, as when working-class families are transferred to new housing estates.

The findings concerning middle-class women's motives for working have been similar. Financial considerations and relief from domestic tedium rank highest, with about equal frequency. The increased cost of living and heavy taxation have in some cases made it necessary for wives to supplement the family income to keep up standards. Non-financial motives include the need for company and the desire to practice certain skills, especially when the women have had pre-marriage experience of interesting jobs with social contacts.

It is possible to analyse the various motives for married women to work according to the typology of relations between work and family spheres outlined earlier. Non-financial motives such as the intrinsic satisfaction derived from work or the desire to practice skills would be associated with the extension pattern. The need for company or pocket money for extras would indicate a middling pattern of neutrality. But the motives of economic necessity or desire to gain relief from domestic tedium show a strong element of opposition.

Effects in work sphere

The employment of part-time women workers involves more work in other respects, for example, extra staff may be needed in personnel, wages and medical departments of firms. Absenteeism is greater among women workers, making supervision and production more difficult. There is a greater tendency for working women to leave their jobs, though the study by Jephcott and her colleagues of a Bermondsey factory revealed that women left their work not because of domestic duties but because of improved opportunities elsewhere.[27] Part-timers who stayed at least six months were likely to achieve a longer service with the company than full-timers.

Seear investigated the employment, training and careers of women in industry.[28] She found that 'the majority of women . . . are required to perform semi-skilled and unskilled jobs, a situation which is individually frustrating and wasteful in terms of national labour resources'. The jobs women are employed in are also those most likely to be modified or eliminated by technological change, making it necessary to prepare them for less routine work. Only one woman in about twenty is employed in a managerial capacity,

[27] P. Jephcott *et al.*, *op. cit.*
[28] N. Seear, *The Position of Women in Industry*, Research Paper 11, Royal Commission on Trade Unions and Employers' Associations (HMSO, 1968).

however, and there is reluctance to train and promote women. Women manual workers' average earnings are approximately half of men's, though this will no doubt change as the policy of equal pay is increasingly implemented.

Effects in family sphere

Wives who earn money by going out to work are more economically independent of their husbands than non-working wives. Greater equality in the occupational sphere between husbands and wives also seems to lead to greater equality in family decision-making. Thus Heer found that in Irish families, both in the working class and in the middle class, the working wife exerts more influence in family decision-making than the non-working wife.[29]

A study by Fogarty and his colleagues focused originally on women in top jobs, but extended both to women's opportunities in professional and graduate work generally and to the relations between family patterns and work careers.[30] Although the authors do not develop a theory of family patterns and work they use the concepts of salience, commitment and integration to move in this direction. Salience refers to the degree to which people attach importance to, and gain satisfaction from, different areas of their lives. Individuals vary in the degree of commitment they have to the idea of women working outside the home at all. The concept of integration is used to define the range of ways in which men as well as women combine the spheres of work and family. The authors believe that commitment is the key concept in determining women's choice of family patterns and/or work. They distinguish: non-commitment, where the woman is quite happy to accept the domestic role and to return to a career if at all only when it is convenient all round to do so; secondary commitment, where the woman wants to have a career, but accepts that this must be secondary to the requirements of her husband's career; and full commitment, where the woman pursues her career with involvement equal to that of her husband and believes that conflicts should be worked out on the basis of joint optimization.

[29] D. M. Heer, 'Dominance and the Working Wife', Social Forces, May 1958.
[30] M. P. Fogarty, Sex, Career and Family (Allen and Unwin, 1971); see also Political and Economic Planning, Women in Top Jobs (Allen and Unwin, 1971).

CHAPTER 5

Industry and Social Stratification

SOCIAL stratification means the division of members of a society into levels or strata that are united by some common attitude or characteristic.[1] Stratification is not a sub-system of society in the same sense as the economy, education or the family system; rather, it is a generalized aspect of the structure of all complex social systems. Nevertheless, it is possible to examine the relationship between social stratification as it is manifest in the sphere of industry and in the wider community. As we have seen with previous inter-institutional relationships, the process is reciprocal.

THE INFLUENCE OF INDUSTRY ON THE STRATIFICATION SYSTEM

Social stratification in modern industrial societies takes two major forms: class and status. Other forms of stratification, such as estates and castes, are not applicable. There is a large and controversial literature on matters connected with social class and status.[2] 'Class' is generally used to denote divisions of people according to their economic position in society, whether they are conscious of that position or not. 'Social status' represents not a division of society but rather a gradation of positions determined by a variety of factors including, but not limited to, economic ones. Historically the concept of class was an important feature of Karl Marx's theory of society, laying emphasis on successive class struggles between owners and non-owners of the means of production, while Max Weber drew attention to another type of

[1] E. V. Schneider, *Industrial Sociology* (New York: McGraw-Hill, 1969), p. 418.
[2] A useful review is contained in T. B. Bottomore's *Classes in Modern Society* (Allen and Unwin, 1965); see also K. Prandy, *Professional Employees* (Faber, 1965), especially Chapter 2.

stratification deriving from the recognition of status which may cut across class structure.

The industrial basis of the stratification system in the wider society is clearly implied in the concept of social classes. Marxists believe that modern industrial societies are divided into two major social classes according to ownership (capitalist class) or non-ownership (working class) of capital or property. Others who accept that there is a class division in society treat it more widely as a division between those with and without power, irrespective of whether that power is economic or not.[3] In the latter case it then becomes a matter of contention whether the non-economic power is in fact associated with economic position, that is, to what extent there is a generalized elite in society that has superior power or authority (legitimated power) in all social spheres.

The link between industry and stratification by status is weaker, mainly because of the wider range of bases for imputing status. If status situation is determined by a specific, positive or negative, social estimation of honour,[4] then it is clear that factors beyond economic and non-economic power and authority can be used to define status—such factors as consumption of goods, education, family background, and so on. However, this does not mean that no connection can be traced between such bases for ascribing status and economic position itself. As in the case of the influence of industry on the family, its influence on the stratification system may be a direct one via economic power and authority position in industry, or an indirect one via the spillover of status in industry into status in the community and the link between market situation and life style.

In Britain official statistics published by the Registrar-General describe 'social class' and 'socio-economic group' in terms of occupation. Non-academic research bodies often use an economic classification that is intended to identify life-styles typical of income groups rather than occupation, though it must be remembered that income is largely based on occupation. A survey by Kahan and others showed that, when a sample of the British public was asked what sort of people it regarded as belonging to the middle and working classes, 61% gave occupational characteristics for the middle class and 74% for the working class.[5] A number of studies both in Britain and America indicate that people tend to put them-

[3] For example, R. Dahrendorf, *Class and Class Conflict in Industrial Society* (Routledge, 1959).

[4] H. H. Gerth and C. W. Mills, *From Max Weber* (Routledge, 1948), p. 187.

[5] M. Kahan et al., 'On the Analytical Division of Social Class', *British Journal of Sociology*, June 1966.

selves in a higher (or sometimes lower) social class as compared with the official rating of their occupation or with the assessment of an interviewer.[6] These subjective judgments reflect a desire on the part of some individuals to identify with a stratum in society other than that in which their occupational membership puts them.

Three studies throw light on the factors that lead some people to emphasize their class position and others their status and generally to take a 'class' or a 'status' view of society. Lockwood's account of *The Blackcoated Worker* shows that although the clerk is, in class terms, 'proletarian', he usually identifies himself with the middle class.[7] It is the work situation of the clerk, rather than his market-determined income, that gives the clue to his 'class-consciousness' and his negative attitude towards unionization. A subsequent article by Goldthorpe and Lockwood examines the phenomenon of 'working-class affluence'.[8] By separating out the economic, relational and normative changes in working-class life, they conclude that, despite the economic progress of the working class in relation to the middle class, the gulf between the two remains very wide. They maintain that there is little basis for the thesis of *embourgeoisement* in the sense of the large-scale assimilation of manual workers and their families to middle-class life-styles: status goals seem much less in evidence than economic goals. Finally, Prandy concludes from his study of scientists and engineers that those who are in positions of authority tend to accept the 'status' view of stratification that they are part of a graded hierarchy, while those who do not share in the exercise of authority tend to have attitudes of a more class type.[9]

Studies of occupational status

As we have seen, stratification by social class is based on objective economic position, while stratification by status is concerned with finer and sometimes non-economic gradations. The question of whether those individuals objectively assigned

[6] British enquiries include a poll by the British Institute of Public Opinion showing that 47% of a sample of the general population assigned themselves to 'the middle classes', G. D. H. Cole, *Studies in Class Structure* (Routledge, 1955), p. 79; Goldthorpe *et al.*, list other studies giving lower proportions of middle-class 'identifiers', and they warn against accepting figures based on different methods of sampling and of establishing self-ratings, *The Affluent Worker in the Class Structure* (Cambridge University Press, 1969), p. 174.

[7] D. Lockwood, *The Blackcoated Worker* (Allen and Unwin, 1958).

[8] J. H. Goldthorpe and D. Lockwood, 'Affluence and the British Class Structure', *Sociological Review*, July 1963.

[9] K. Prandy, *op. cit.*

by occupation or economic position to a certain class agree with that placement has led to the term 'false class consciousness' being used to describe those who identify with the 'wrong' class. With status stratification, however, the whole matter is far more open. Many enquiries have been concerned with the differential statuses that certain occupations are thought to have. Some of these enquiries are described as relating to occupational 'prestige', but it seems better to use 'status' to refer to a position within a group or society and reserve 'prestige' for something more personal that an individual brings to a status.

Probably the best-known British study of the social grading of occupations is the one by Hall and Jones.[10] They asked 1,400 people to rank 30 occupations in order of social grading, that is, they asked for their informants' views of what they thought was the general opinion. They concluded that there was no major difference in regard to the grading of selected occupations. The difference in average judgment was likely to be greater in grading occupations in the central region of the occupational scale than at the top or bottom, and there was a tendency for judgments about the social status of selected occupations to become more variable with the lower occupational status of informants.

Young and Willmott confirmed this last point in their study of the social grading of occupations by manual workers.[11] They found a considerable measure of dissensus among these workers, who tended to grade occupations according to their usefulness to society, putting manual workers above non-manual. The authors commented that 'in future enquiries it would be as well to ask people not only for their view of the general opinion about the standing of jobs but also for their own personal opinion'. In other words, we need to know the meanings that men attach to their own and each other's actions, in this case the action of judging that certain occupations should be accorded higher status than others.

Criticism of studies

Studies of the social grading of occupations may be objected to on the grounds that they force people into making distinctions that they do not normally make. The idea behind most occupational status studies is that occupations are scalable, that is, they can be located on a single scale of high to low according to their

[10] J. Hall and D. Jones, 'Social Grading of Occupations', *British Journal of Sociology*, March 1950.

[11] M. Young and P. Willmott, 'Social Grading by Manual Workers', *British Journal of Sociology*, December 1956.

status. But, as Reiss points out, 'occupational rankings derived from the rating procedure . . . do not yield a unidimensional scale for all occupations . . . there are good reasons for assuming that status is a multidimensional phenomenon and that there is more than a single dimension to most of the conventional indicators of status'.[12]

One reason for the lack of universal agreement about the status of occupations may be that status is only one way of classifying occupations—the vertical way. Morris and Murphy have suggested the term 'situs' to describe a more horizontal classification by equally valued functional categories.[13] The use of the situs dimension provides us with a technique to assess the relative effect of *type* of work, as well as of class or status, on attitudes and behaviour. This is reflected in the growing interest in sociological studies of particular occupations, rather than of the hypothetically common experiences of individuals at a certain class or status level.

Status congruency

Differences in judgments of status may be partly explained by analysing the different sources of status. A job can carry status because of the rewards (economic or psychological) attached to it, because of prestige, authority, or functional importance.[14] These four sources of status may be congruent or not. If a person is high on status in one respect he will tend to feel relative deprivation if he is low on status in other respects. This leads to a 'strain towards congruency' of status attributes. This also operates on the group level—if one job is better than another by most values of a group there will be efforts by the generally higher-ranking group to bring all the status factors into line.[15]

There is the wider question of the extent to which status differences in the work milieu carry over into non-work life. A job with high status can help the entry into such things as golf clubs or fraternal associations because the individual's status is held to be 'portable'. On the other hand, the motivation for some non-work activities involving positions of status, for example, in religious life or local government, may be the seeking of compensation for lack of status in occupational life.

[12] A. J. Reiss, *Occupations and Social Status* (Glencoe: Free Press), 1961.

[13] R. T. Morris and R. J. Murphy, 'The Situs Dimension in Occupational Stratification', *American Sociological Review*, April 1959.

[14] R. J. Pellegrin and F. L. Bates, 'Congruity and Incongruity of Status Attributes within Occupations and Work Positions', *Social Forces*, October 1959.

[15] G. C. Homans, *Sentiments and Activities* (Routledge, 1962), p. 93f.

THE INFLUENCE OF THE STRATIFICATION
SYSTEM ON INDUSTRY

Industrial enterprises, collectively and individually, have a system of stratification that has internal and external aspects. Internally, the division of various types of workers and managers into strata may be held to be functional or dysfunctional for the enterprise or the industrial system as a whole. Externally, it is possible to trace the ways in which status stratification in the community influences the status privileges that are accorded to certain individuals in their occupational roles. These two aspects are analytically distinct, but in practice merge; as Bergel puts it, every stratification system finally correlates status and occupation.[16]

Just as there are social classes or status groups in society at large, so within industrial enterprises there are hierarchical levels of authority to which varying degrees of status are attached. Apart from the role of shareholders in providing capital for some types of industrial enterprise, the various roles in industry are structured by levels of authority, with the chief executive at the top and the ordinary workers at the bottom. What are the reasons for the existence of a stratification system in industry? Defenders of the status system in industry stress the need to recruit managers and technical experts by offering 'appropriate' rewards, including those of high status. Critics of status consciousness in industry point to its divisive consequences, such as failure of communication between strata and (in class terms) the attitudes associated with the recognition of 'two sides of industry', i.e. management and workers.

There is ample evidence of the concern with status in industry on the part of both management and workers. Many managers expect their hours of work and privileges associated with their employment to be sharply distinguished from those of lower grades. A process of social differentiation is often active within a management structure as well as between managers and other employees. Clements, for example, found that senior management positions tended to be filled by men who were of higher social origin and who were even trained for senior management posts at an earlier point in their careers.[17]

Workers show concern for status in different ways. Those who are moved to another job at the same pay but with lower informal

[16] E. E. Bergel, *Social Stratification* (New York: McGraw-Hill, 1962), p. 330.
[17] R. V. Clements, *Managers: A Study of their Careers in Industry* (Allen and Unwin, 1958), p. 95.

status often become deeply resentful.[18] Differences in wage rates between various jobs are also important in establishing status. Workers are often more concerned with how their wages compare with others (the 'differential') than with absolute amounts—hence the difficulty of devising a generally acceptable incomes policy. The difference between shop floor and staff status can be a source of discontent; a survey of apprentices showed that those who were in an intermediate position between being close to staff status and far removed from it were more likely to be irritated by differences in treatment between staff and shop floor workers.[19]

To what extent can status position in the workplace be kept separate from status position outside the workplace? It seems clear that some separation between the two statuses is possible for many workers. The principal factors in this process are the tendency for people no longer to carry the 'marks' of their occupation with them into non-work life, shorter working hours, and the comparative rarity of having work as a central life interest. Divorce between status at work and in the community is, however, more possible in urban than rural areas, because status is ascribed to categories who share clusters of characteristics but with whose component members one does not necessarily interact.[20] That the consumption standards (an obvious 'status attribute') of the working class have become more like those of at least some sections of the middle class cannot be denied, although social strata within industry and the authority relationships on which these are based have remained broadly unchanged. As Goldthorpe and his colleagues remark, 'despite his affluence, the worker's experience of the social divisions of the workplace, of the power and remoteness of management, and of his own inconsiderable chances of ever being anything but a manual wage-earner all generally dispose him to think of himself as a member of the class of 'ordinary workers', and to seek collective rather than individualistic solutions to his problems'.[21]

Stratification theory and industry

Contributions to stratification theory in Britain have largely been consequences of investigating particular problems. British sociologists have concentrated on concrete issues such as the

---

[18] J. A. C. Brown, *The Social Psychology of Industry* (Penguin, 1954), p. 140.

[19] T. S. Chivers and S. R. Parker, 'The Apprentice Technician and his Job', *Industrial Society*, October 1966.

[20] R. Frankenberg, *Communities in Britain* (Penguin, 1966), p. 263.

[21] J. H. Goldthorpe *et al.*, *The Affluent Worker: Political Attitudes and Behaviour* (Cambridge University Press, 1968), p. 78.

meaning of 'working-class affluence' and the correlates of different types of working-class situation.[22] For a consideration of more theoretical issues involved in stratification we must turn to American sociologists, who have been carrying on a somewhat polemical debate on the subject for the past quarter of a century. Much of this debate turns on whether stratification is 'inevitable' in any society, and therefore relates more to the philosophy of stratification than to its sociology. But the exchange of views has also dealt with some substantive issues in 'macro' sociology and at some points is relevant to the question of stratification in industry. Huaco has recently surveyed the whole series of exchanges, and the following is a summary of his article.[23]

In 1945 Davis and Moore first put forward their theory of stratification, in which they argued that there is a 'universal necessity which calls forth stratification in any social system'. On the one hand, they maintained, different positions have different degrees of functional importance for societal preservation or survival; on the other hand, the amount of talent and training available in the population is scarce. So the system attaches greater rewards to the functionally more important positions in order to insure that the individuals with greatest talent and training occupy these positions. In 1948 Davis added the modification that mobility of the more talented and trained individuals into the more highly rewarded positions is prevented partially by status ascription through the family.

In 1953 Tumin questioned the logical status of the notion of differential functional importance as being unmeasurable and intuitive. He also questioned the differential scarcity of personnel as an adequate determinant of stratification. He argued that in practice most stratification systems artificially restrict the development of whatever potential talent and skill may exist in the population. Davis replied, agreeing that stratification restricted talent and training, but maintaining that the 1948 version of his theory had met this objection by explaining ascription in terms of the role of the family. In a reply to Davis, Tumin further challenged the necessity of 'unequal rewards' by suggesting the

[22] For example, the proletarian (conscious of his membership of the working class and its traditions of struggle), the deferential (thinking largely in terms of prestige and accepting the leadership of his 'betters'), and the privatized (concerned with money and possessions and with no real class consciousness), D. Lockwood, 'Sources of Variation in Working Class Images of Society', *Sociological Review*, November 1966.

[23] G. A. Huaco, 'The Functionalist Theory of Stratification: Two Decades of Controversy', in M. M. Tumin (ed.), *Readings in Social Stratification* (Englewood Cliffs: Prentice-Hall, 1970).

feasibility of 'functional equivalents', for example, intrinsic job satisfaction and social service may be adequate motivations 'for seeking one's appropriate position and fulfilling it conscientiously'.

In succeeding years a number of criticisms and rejoinders were made by various writers, notably including Buckley and Stinchcombe. Huaco attempts to sort out those portions of the Davis-Moore theory 'which have been destroyed by the critics from the more solid and promising fragments'. He believes that the postulate of differential functional importance is a fallacy, there being no evidence that different positions make different degrees of contribution to societal preservation or survival. Also, the assumption that societies whose stratification systems approach a pure achievement order have greater survival or endurance than most ascriptive societies is probably false. Nevertheless, three remaining parts of the theory seem to Huaco to be valid: (1) unequal rewards attached to different positions are a cause of the mobility of individuals into certain positions, (2) the existence and operation of the institution of the family is a cause of status ascription, and (3) differential scarcity of qualified personnel is a cause of 'stratification' (unequal rewards attached to different positions).

Originally formulated as part of the structural-functional explanation of the nature of society, the Davis-Moore theory of stratification has thus effectively been modified to the point where its claims are restricted to the formulation of propositions about the effect of structural features of society on the attitudes and behaviour of its members. Social action theorists have not developed a theory of stratification, although it is not difficult to see the general lines that this would take. The division of society into strata is problematic. Strata in society or in industry do not exist 'out there' separately from actors' definition of the situation. The existence of stratification in a society ultimately rests on a majority of its members legitimizing the differences in authority attached to the various strata.[24] In particular, the superordinate position of the higher stratum (order-givers, managers, leaders) is not possible without the consent of a majority of the lower stratum (order-takers, the managed, the led).

[24] For a discussion of the concept of legitimacy and its application to social organization see A. Fox, *A Sociology of Work in Industry* (Collier-Macmillan, 1971), especially Chapter II.

CHAPTER 6

Industry, the Community and the Polity

IN this final chapter dealing with the relation between industry and other sub-systems of society we shall consider under the broad heading of 'the community and the polity' some of those aspects of society not covered in previous chapters. By 'the community' we mean a continuous geographical area in which mutually dependent groups act together to satisfy their needs through a common set of organizations and institutions.[1] By 'the polity' we mean the sub-system of society oriented to the generation and allocation of power, the relation of the polity and government being conceived as approximately parallel to that of the economy and business.[2]

INDUSTRY AND THE COMMUNITY

Industry influences the community

Industry, in the broad sense of technology, economic enterprises and persons associated with these, has pervasive effects on the communities it serves and from which it draws its resources. These effects may be considered under three heads: values, physical effects on the community, and purposive attempts of industrial interest groups to influence society.

Industry feeds into the community people whose personal characteristics reflect their experiences at work. Just as Weber showed that, in addition to technical possibilities and material conditions, the appropriate values were necessary to the develop-

[1] W. A. Anderson and F. B. Parker, *Society: Its Organization and Operation* (New Jersey: Van Nostrand, 1964), p. 102.
[2] Talcott Parsons, *Structure and Process in Modern Societies* (Glencoe: Free Press, 1960, p. 42.

ment and maintenance of traditional capitalist society, so a certain set of basic minimum values are necessary to the maintenance of modern capitalism. People generally must accept their position both in the industrial structure and in the wider social structure. Because production is dependent on consumption, they must be persuaded to buy the goods and services that industry is capable of producing—industry has the function both of making the goods and of identifying and encouraging the desires for them.[3] This involves values at the 'macro' level of society, but there are also more local and specific changes in values brought about by changes in industry. For example, the effect on Oxford of the growth of the motor-car industry may be cited: its change to a high-wage town led to alterations in old-established ideas about the informal hierarchy of jobs among the wage-earners.[4]

Industry has certain physical effects on the communities in which it operates. In various ways the community feels the effects of what is happening in industry. Where towns are heavily dependent on a single industry or firm, the fortunes of that industry or firm will determine whether the town prospers or declines. The establishment of new industries in an area will affect the total number and spatial distribution of workers. To take the South Wales industrial area as an example, new employment regions have taken over from the small, relatively independent mining and tinplate towns. These new regions tend to have new centres of employment, between which are areas of comparative industrial stagnation from which work forces for the new centres are drawn.

The purposive attempts of industrial interest groups to influence society may be seen in their efforts to make a favourable impression on public opinion. Advertising, in addition to its manifest function of promoting the products of the enterprise, has also the latent function of promoting the enterprise itself, a function that is more specifically performed by public relations departments.[5] Many large firms organize parties of visitors to tour their establishments. On the side of labour, the 'public relations' activities of trade unions are generally less in evidence, apart from the appearance of union leaders on television to put their case in disputes with employers. Unlike the majority of daily newspapers that tend to put the employers' or a 'national' point of view, union journals circulate mainly among union members.

[3] J. K. Galbraith, *The Affluent Society* (Penguin, 1962), p. 122; see also *The New Industrial State* (Hamish Hamilton, 1967).
[4] J. M. Mogey, *Family and Neighbourhood* (Oxford: University Press, 1956), p. 5.
[5] In the case of 'prestige' advertising this function becomes a manifest one.

Another, and more theoretical way of looking at the mutual influences of industry and the community is to identify types of industry-community relations. Although there are separate economic interest groups within industry such as those of commerce, industry, agriculture, finance, and organized labour, for some purposes most of these groups (excluding labour) may be regarded as one wider interest group that interacts with the community, itself a composite of various interests. Form and Miller have suggested that there are five types of relationship between this wide economic interest group and the community:[6]

(1) *business-dictated* is where employers dictate working hours without much concern for their effect on home life, and workers must accommodate their family life to industrial operations (this is likely in a one-industry town with a limited labour market or an industry-dominated town with weak or unorganized labour),

(2) *business-dominated* is similar to the above, but management negotiates certain conditions of work with the union, while retaining work rules and hours as a management prerogative (likely where management authority is strong, with a fairly strong union but some surplus labour),

(3) *labour-mediated*: unions attempt to share management's right to determine working hours, and there may be labour-management councils (strong labour union, industry dependent on local skilled labour),

(4) *equilibrium*: unions are strong, and so are other community influences, for example, civic associations, management decisions have to be considered in the light of their effect on the local community (highly integrated community), and

(5) *family-mediated*: family values are dominant (family ownership of the enterprise, religious or co-operative communities).

These types of relationship between industry and community have been worked out in connection with American industrial and social conditions and need to be modified if applied to Britain. Thus the business-dictated pattern would be hard to find in Britain, except in the sense that certain types of workers are motivated by high pay or a sense of vocation to subordinate their family and leisure lives to the demands of work.[7] The authors also suggest that there are four approaches to industry-community relations: (1) *structural-functional*, involving social ramifications

[6] W. H. Form and D. C. Miller, *Industry, Labor and Community* (New York: Harper, 1960).

[7] Examples of manual workers in these circumstances are those engaged in oil drilling, tunnelling or distant-water fishing, and of non-manual workers, some business executives, social work or medical personnel.

of industry into other sub-systems, (2) *compensation*, in which industry is seen as a source of sociability not possible in the local community,[8] (3) the *welfare* approach to community affairs, industry taking part as a responsible partner, and (4) *power*, industry being the major source of power affecting the community.

The community influences industry

The above theoretical approaches to industry-community relations may be illustrated by examples of ways in which community norms and values exert influence on industrial structure and behaviour. Deferring consideration of the more political influences until the next section, we may concentrate on cases in which management has to adjust its practices to the social and cultural realities of communities in which it operates.[9] The processes of adjustment between the needs and attitudes of workers and the behaviour that management requires of them are not easy to trace; the extent to which one side accommodates to the other is a function of the power relations between them. Adjustment on the side of industry (i.e. management) may be seen typically in the cases of minority groups of employees, of which juveniles, women and immigrant workers may be taken as examples.

As we saw in Chapter 3, there are various ways in which management accepts the fact that some juvenile workers need to complete their education by taking part in day-release, sandwich and other training courses. The community's idea of appropriate education takes precedence over at least some employers' aim of maximizing profits from employing juvenile labour. In the case of women workers, many factory managers have found it necessary to make special arrangements concerning shifts and to accept 'controlled absenteeism' when the women want time off to look after their domestic duties.

The employment of immigrant workers, particularly coloured

---

[8] This view was put forward by Elton Mayo , *The Social Problems of an Industrial Civilization* (Harvard: University Press, 1945), to stress the importance of group life in industry.

[9] It will be noted that in this formulation 'management' has taken the place of 'industry' as interacting with the community. We can analyse organizations either in terms of 'system' problems, regarding human action as a reflection of system needs, or in terms of the meanings that actors within organizations attach to their own actions and those of others (D. Silverman, *The Theory of Organizations* (Heinemann, 1970), p. 41). The substitution of 'management' for 'industry' represents a shift from system to action analysis. A parallel substitution would be 'community interest groups' for 'the community'.

workers, poses a different kind of problem for industry.[10] The degree of integration of coloured workers into the labour force is part of the wider issue of the integration of coloured citizens into the community at large. This means that some employers are conscious of a conflict between the policies they feel they have to pursue as employers and those which, as citizens, they feel they would like to see followed. Sometimes they will give reasons showing how it is uneconomic for them to employ coloured labour when whites are available, but they are uncomfortable about the implications of this if all employers were to do the same.

In various ways the community feels the effect of events and changes that take place in industry and sometimes seeks to exert influence on these. Labour-management relations are usually felt to be mainly the concern of employers, unions and government, but when strikes, lockouts or redundancies occur a wider public is interested because of the plight of unemployed workers and the consequent effect on the economic well-being of the community. On the national level the wages and salaries paid to employees and the prices charged to consumers for goods and services have become of interest to those other than persons directly affected, as part of a wider concern with the problem of inflation. On the role-person level, the social life of employees has a bearing upon industrial organization, efficiency and morale. It is now a common-place of industrial sociology that attitudes and behaviour in industry—such as absenteeism, labour turnover, pressures for minimum or maximum effort—cannot be explained by reference to conditions in industry alone, but are also dependent on norms, values, roles and expectations in non-industrial spheres.

INDUSTRY AND THE POLITY

Industry and political influence

Industry operates in a societal environment and has certain relations of power with that environment. Power is generated and exercised within industrial organizations and also outside these, the latter area being our chief concern here. The forms of influence that industry has in the political sphere may be divided into two types: organized group and dual-role individual. In seeking to influence central and local government policies, representatives of industrial interests may form themselves into organized pressure

[10] P. L. Wright, *The Coloured Worker in British Industry* (Oxford University Press, 1968); S. Patterson, *Immigrants in Industry* (Oxford University Press, 1968).

groups, while the personnel of industrial undertakings may also have part-time political roles through which their economic interests may be promoted.

Pressure groups are part of the modern political scene: they have been defined as organized groups possessing both formal structure and real common interests, in so far as they seek to influence the process of government.[11] One of the major forms of pressure group is the economic, including employers, manufacturers and traders on the one hand, and organized labour (trade unions and professional associations) on the other. Although in recent years the Labour Party has extended its appeal to groups on its right and the Conservative Party its appeal to groups on its left, each has core support from the trade union movement in the one case and business interests in the other. These pressure groups operate through processes of consultation and advice. Some references to consultation appear in statutes but mostly it has little formal expression in the outward structure of government except by means of advisory committees. In addition, the general strategy of pressure groups in seeking to influence decision-making bodies is carried out through tactics of influencing public opinion by petition, advertising, public meetings, the activities of individual M.Ps. and those of lobbyists.

The ability of members of industry (usually management members) to influence political policies by direct participation in government is an aspect of control by interlocking elites in industry and government.[12] Retired ministers in Conservative governments often, and in Labour governments occasionally, take seats on the boards of top industrial companies and banks.[13] The interlocking of industrial and government control was at its peak in wartime when leading industrialists moved into government posts to operate wartime controls, but in the post-war period the nationalized industries have provided many opportunities for top appointments of industrialists and trade union leaders. At the level of local government, it is significant that employers, managers and professional people are over-represented four times on local councils in proportion to their numbers in the general popula-

[11] J. D. Stewart, *British Pressure Groups* (Oxford: Clarendon Press, 1958), p. 1; see also A. Potter, *Organized Groups in British National Politics* (Faber, 1961).

[12] This exacerbates the problems facing any government intending to take measures opposed to business interests. 'The control by business of large and crucially important areas of economic life makes it extremely *difficult* for governments to impose upon it policies to which it is firmly opposed.' R. Miliband, *The State in Capitalist Society* (Weidenfeld and Nicolson, 1969), p. 147.

[13] M. Barratt Brown, 'The Controllers', *Universities and Left Review*, Autumn 1958.

tion.[14] It is not suggested that there is normally anything improper in combining the roles of businessman and councillor, although occasionally individuals are accused of taking advantage of their public office for personal gain.

Political and legal constraints on industry

Most of the relationships between industry and other sub-systems of society that we have considered in previous chapters and in the first part of this chapter have shown industry to have a greater effect on other sub-systems than vice versa. In the case of the political-legal sphere this is not so. Although the *degree* of control of industry deemed desirable has been hotly debated, there is today no question that *some* controls are necessary to maintain economic and social stability and ensure some kind of reconciliation between economic and other social interests. Legal regulation of industry has been clearly established, but there is still controversy as to how far it should go.

The role of government (or more broadly of the state) in industry may be considered under a number of headings: as controller, regulator, promoter, entrepreneur, and planner.[15] The state has acquired economic functions in a haphazard and piecemeal fashion, so it is hardly surprising that these are exercised by many different bodies: central departments, local authorities, independent public boards, commissions and corporations, and even private bodies that have been specially endowed with public powers. The ways in which direct government control of industry is exercised include budgetary policy, discriminatory taxation, hire-purchase controls, the control of public investment and of the distribution of industry.

In its role as regulator the state provides a framework for the orderly operation of business enterprise. Some of the main ways in which it does this are by incorporation of companies, registration of trade unions and employers' associations, measures for the protection of the consumer and the investor, control of restrictive trading agreements and of wages and conditions of work. The state also attempts to sponsor and promote the interests of industry in various ways. It promotes industrial and agricultural research, and is interested in improving industrial productivity and

---

[14] L. Moss and S. R. Parker, *The Local Government Councillor* (HMSO, 1967).
[15] These roles correspond to chapter headings in J. W. Grove's *Government and Industry in Britain* (Longman, 1962), where these matters are discussed in detail. For a general, if controversial, overview of the relationship between the state and the industrial system see J. K. Galbraith, *The New Industrial State* (Penguin, 1969), especially Chapters 26 and 27.

efficiency. Public ownership and regulation plays a part in industrial reorganization, and there is regulated marketing of certain products through marketing boards. Other measures of direct support for trade include tariffs and other protection for domestic industries and the promotion of exports. The government is also interested in improving industrial relations and provides employment services, industrial training and technical education.

In its role as entrepreneur the state directly participates in the economy in four ways. It is an important purchaser of goods and services for its own use; it is a large employer (about one million out of a working population of 24 millions); it exercises a considerable direct influence on employment in other parts of the public services which it finances and supervises but does not manage; and it produces and trades on a limited scale for its own use. Finally, as planner the government extends its role as controller. The machinery for directing and guiding the economy has traditionally been highly decentralized but, irrespective of differences between the main political parties, the economic difficulties facing the country have led to a greater role for central government in planning industrial development and activity.

Industrial relations and the law

The piecemeal and somewhat reluctant intervention of the state in the affairs of industry is paralleled by a similar piecemeal and reluctant intervention of the law in the field of industrial relations. As Wedderburn remarks, the law tends to make its appearance only when things go radically wrong.[16] The reasons for this must be sought in the forms in which collective bargaining between employers and unions has developed in Britain and in the history of trade unionism. Collective bargaining has been essentially voluntary and covered by very few decisions of the judges because it was rarely brought into any court.

In 1971, however, after an abortive attempt by the previous Labour government to introduce legislation, the Conservative government passed the Industrial Relations Act. Its chief provisions include the right given to workers to belong to a registered trade union, as well as not to belong to any kind of union; the holding of written collective agreements to be legally enforceable contracts unless they contain an express provision to the contrary; legal protection against unfair dismissal for employees with two or more years' service; and the definition of a number of 'unfair industrial practices' (mostly circumstances in which strikes are

[16] K. W. Wedderburn, *The Worker and the Law* (MacGibbon and Kee, 1966), p. 13.

called or other industrial action taken), infringement of which may lead to heavy penalties being imposed by the National Industrial Relations Court (equivalent to the High Court).[17]

Apart from the vexed question of industrial relations, there are two main areas which fall within the province of labour law. These are (1) the employment relationship between worker and employer, governed by common law and more recently by the Contracts of Employment Act, 1963 and the Redundancy Payments Act, 1965, and (2) the statutory control of certain conditions of employment, including the level of wages in 'wages council' industries where it is difficult to organize workers in unions, and safety and related conditions at work.

Occupation and political behaviour

It is possible to trace an association between type of occupation and political attitudes and behaviour. The data again are often in terms of social class or socio-economic group. Of the working class about two-thirds usually vote Labour, and of the middle class 70–85% vote Conservative. Although Labour Party members are generally distributed occupationally in proportion to Labour voters, more Conservative Party members come from non-manual groups in proportion to Conservative voters.[18] In both parties manual workers are not represented among the leaders in proportion to their numbers among the electors. An occupational analysis of the 1970 Parliament showed that whereas manual workers (about 60% of the working population) provided 26% of Labour M.Ps. they provided only 1% of Conservative M.Ps.[19] Professional employees were heavily over-represented among M.Ps. of both parties.

Studies of particular localities and occupational groups supplement the findings on a national scale. In Derby it was found that there was very little difference between the political participation of non-manual and skilled manual workers, but unskilled manual workers participated less often.[20] It is reasonable to suppose that greater autonomy and participation in work decisions predisposes a worker to greater interest in political matters. Also, particular

[17] For a sympathetic interpretation of the aims of the Act see J. Henderson, *A Guide to the Industrial Relations Bill* (The Industrial Society, 1971); and for a critical assessment *Reason* (Trades Union Congress, 1970).

[18] J. Blondel, *Voters, Parties and Leaders* (Penguin, 1963), p. 91.

[19] D. Butler and M. Pinto-Duschinsky, *The British General Election of 1970* (Macmillan, 1970), p. 302.

[20] T. Cauter and J. Downham, *The Communication of Ideas* (Chatto and Windus, 1954).

occupations seem to be associated with political as well as industrial militancy, such as car workers and dockers. Types of work that feature occupational communities with a shared ideology tend to be associated with left-wing attitudes and voting. Thus Cannon found that compositors, who earned above average wages, tended more often to vote Labour than other members of the skilled working class.[21]

A number of studies have investigated the effect of plant size and of knowing one's boss on a personal basis as factors influencing political attitudes and behaviour. Nordlinger found that, although larger factory size is related to Left voting, when plant size is controlled for, face-to-face contact between worker and employer is not *directly* related to Conservative voting.[22] Ingham came to much the same conclusion from his inquiry among Bradford workers and offers a plausible explanation: 'Given a labour force whose community structure fosters left wing political values, increased worker-management interaction may, in fact, lead to an intensification of these values by virtue of the fact that the roles and activities of the "other side" or "them" become more visible.'[23]

[21] I. C. Cannon, 'Ideology and Occupational Community: A Study of Compositors', *Sociology*, May 1967.

[22] E. A. Nordlinger, *The Working-Class Tories* (MacGibbon and Kee, 1967).

[23] G. K. Ingham, 'Plant Size: Political Attitudes and Behaviour', *Sociological Review*, July 1969.

CHAPTER 7

Perspectives on Organizations

THE experience of social organization is universal. We are born into one kind—the family, educated in another—the school, work in yet another—the firm, and may spend our leisure in a variety of others—the pub, the sports club, the theatre. Organizations provide the social fabric for many of the relationships in which we engage and the choices we make. Most of the time we are not aware of the very complexity of such a fabric except where it impinges on us. Most of the time too we are only half aware that, of the variety of organizations of which we are a part, some are very different from others. What is tolerated in the family setting may not be so in work or elsewhere. Behaviour at work often differs radically from behaviour in leisure settings. These differences may find expression in the kinds of views held and the behaviour considered appropriate for different contexts. At a commonsense level this is clearly recognized and people vary their actions and behaviour to fit the particular context of a relationship. Organizations, then, are part of our everyday experience—if only because they act as constraints on our behaviour. In what ways they differ and their significance, especially in relation to the world of work, are the issues to be examined.

Sociologists have never been content to analyse organizations from one basic perspective, which is not surprising in view of the historical origins of sociology. In the course of its development sociology has been influenced by two basic models of the social world: the world as a *biological organism*, the claim that natural systems are the same as social systems; and the world as a sphere of *rational action*, as man interpreting the meaning he gives to his own action choices. The social system approach and the social action perspective may be associated with Durkheim and Weber

* See Dawes, analysis.

respectively, and have tended to parallel each other in their development.

Durkheim, functionalism and the social systems approach

For Durkheim the biological analogy centred upon those elements which enabled the survival and evolution of a social species—a society. The organic nature of society meant explaining what held it together—the source and nature of consensus and social order. Durkheim classified types of society according to how social relationships within them had become segmented. In societies characterized by mechanistic solidarity individuals experienced their own behaviour as part of a 'total framework' and their choices tended to be 'mechanical', i.e. governed by that framework. With industrialization, increased population and a higher 'density' or frequency of interaction occurs. Division of labour creates both the segmentation of social relationships and the necessity of interdependence amongst different parts of society. Organic solidarity characterizes societies in which action choices are more open-ended and people more self aware. As societies move towards organic solidarity the sources of integration become important—the moral order underpinned by the law and attachment to reference groups, for Durkheim, provided such sources. Durkheim saw the possibility of the breakdown of social organization, the state of *anomie* in which people became detached from their reference groups and the moral order disintegrated. Anomie, for Durkheim, was an abnormal form of the division of labour, a symptom of a diseased social world.

Durkheim's concern with the social world as a biological organism led him to diagnose rather than prescribe solutions. It also depended upon the truth of fundamental propositions about the nature of the social world. These propositions underpin the classical functionalist approach and the contemporary 'system' models in sociology and support the general functionalist explanation of society. Understanding these propositions is a central part of grasping the essential differences between sociologists in their approach to organizational theory. These propositions are broadly as follows:

(1) Society has certain basic needs, the prime one being the need to survive and maintain itself.

(2) These needs may be treated as goals and regulate the structure of society.

(3) The structure of society is differentiated according to the functions performed by the different elements in relation to the goal of survival.

(4) The most useful analytical construct through which to identify basic societal needs and structural elements is that of 'social system'.

(5) The total social system is a society and both organizations and individuals relate to the structure of the system by sharing its basic needs or goals.

These propositions do not of course typify Durkheim; they are claims which have developed since his time. He was well aware of the danger of treating functions as causes—a common failing of contemporary functionalism. He also attempted to link his explanatory categories to the ongoing 'real' or empirical world, the concern being more with the descriptive adequacy of the schema than the logical status of its categories. Contemporary functionalism has moved away from the Durkheim approach and tends to be more formal in the sense of presenting a highly abstract model into which can be fitted a variety of data. Not all functionalists are unaware of the difficulties which result from this deductive approach. Some, like Merton,[1] have suggested that the key point to commence explanation is social relationships which can be anchored in the social fabric. For Merton the expectations or norms which govern such relationships provide the interpretative link between the individual's needs and socially approved behaviour patterns. Others, such as Gouldner,[2] have tried to relate the more general propositions of functionalism to particular problems—such as that of industrial bureaucracy. Another achievement, in a different direction, is the attempt to provide historical and detailed content for the deductive model; Smelser has made the most significant contribution in these terms.[3]

The criticisms of the functionalist approach are many and bear directly on the variety of organizational approaches which cluster around the system construct as a basis for explanation. The more specific criticisms are related to particular organizational models, but it is helpful to identify the more general ones:

1. The concept of 'system' distorts the nature of social reality— the social world is much less coherent and integrated than the concept implies.

2. The claim that social systems have basic needs, like those of natural systems, assumes a too easy transference from the biological to the social world.

[1] R. K. Merton, *Social Theory and Social Structure* (New York: Free Press, 1949).

[2] A. W. Gouldner, *Patterns of Industrial Bureaucracy* (New York: Free Press, 1954); also see 'Organizational Analysis', in R. K. Merton (ed.), *Sociology Today* (New York: Basic Books, 1959).

[3] N. J. Smelser, *Social Change in the Industrial Revolution* (Routledge, 1959).

3. The claim that all systems possess goals imputes a teleological status to all institutions and behaviour. Certainly 'purpose' is central to social explanation, but it is doubtful if this can be imputed to all social phenomena.

4. The concept of 'function' is ambiguous. Does it mean 'cause', and why should everything be supposed to have a function to be analysable?

5. Most functionalist analysis is difficult to relate to the 'real' world. Highly abstract categories destroy the interesting and detailed aspects of social life.

6. It is ideologically motivated. The functionalist model is conducive to a conservative stress on social order and political and social consensus. The neglect of conflict as a subject of analysis reinforces this suspicion.

Weber, rationalism and the social action approach

The claims of the general functionalist position are in sharp contrast to the model which has developed in parallel to it—the Weberian view. This maintains that the social world is the sphere of rational action and that social explanation consists of interpreting the meaning man gives to his own behaviour and choices. For Weber patterns of 'legitimacy' were the key to understanding industrial society. What was the social basis of the belief in legal-rational authority—how was a constellation of values achieved? For Weber the answer was illustrated by the protestant ethic—thrift and worldly asceticism were directly linked to the growth of the acquisitive capitalist society. The desire for earthly confirmation of heavenly success lead the Calvinist to reinvest his time and resources in his business—the early Calvinist was the prototype of the capitalist entrepreneur. However, over time, this ethic lost its religious significance. The secularization process was, according to Weber, an outcome of the growth of rationalism. Industrial society was unique in that it developed a value system centred upon the pursuit of knowledge and the application of scientific principles to the natural and social worlds. Weber was ambivalent about what kind of society would result from this process, but did not exclude the possibility of one of total boredom and total terror. People could lose their individuality and their freedom. The bureaucrat could replace the politician and the locus of decision-making could become some form of political and social tyranny.

The model of bureaucracy which Weber developed was an illustration of this trend and an examination of the possible organizational form consequent upon the growth of a rational society. Bureaucracy was rational—it depended upon impartial assessment and objective criteria for its functioning. It was characterized by limitation of spheres of authority in which responsibilities were clearly related to organizational position. Communication and information processes followed the hierarchical nature of the authority structure, and rational organization was the key to efficiency. Of course this model has been extensively examined and criticized.[4] Some general weaknesses are worth noting: it tended to focus on formal organizational elements and ignore the wealth of informal friendship patterns and leadership roles; it tended to the view that hierarchical authority was most conducive to efficiency in decision making (it may of course be dysfunctional by inhibiting ideas from flowing freely in relation to any particular problem and creating frustration and distortion amongst those 'low' in the hierarchy). The rules which govern the allocation and exercise of positional responsibilities may themselves be 'ritualized' or turned into ends in themselves. Weber himself was less concerned with how efficient bureaucracy was than with how far it revealed basic trends towards a rational society. Interestingly enough, since Weber's time the popular usage of the concept has become synonymous with inefficiency.

Bureaucracy was the organizational outworking of the rationalism which Weber regarded as the dominant feature of Western capitalism. In developing a model of rational man and a social action perspective, there was the same overall concern with patterns of rationality. As Parsons has observed,[5] Weber's model was more concerned with the rationality of the *means* used to achieve particular ends than with questioning the status of the ends themselves. The rational relationship of means to ends was the ideal type against which action choices could be assessed. Weber distinguished the rational appropriateness of the means chosen to achieve particular objectives or ends from 'affective' action, where the means were chosen on the basis of emotion, and action where the means were governed by tradition or custom. He also recognized that the actual meaning which people give to their own behaviour can be a mixture of these elements and that understanding this component requires both observation and empathy. Weber's focus on a typology of action, asking what meaning people may give to their own behaviour, is the basic axiom of what has become known as the social action perspective,

[4] N. P. Mouzelis, *Organization and Bureaucracy* (Routledge, 1967).
[5] T. Parsons, Introduction to Max Weber's *The Theory of Social and Economic Organization* (New York: Free Press, 1964).

and more broadly the interactionist view of social reality. The general propositions which form the basis of this perspective may be conveniently identified, although as with the functionalist approach these are not limited to any one theorist:

1. Man is not a passive recipient of the external world but is constantly interpreting and shaping its meaning for himself.

2. This interpretative and shaping process distinguishes animal behaviour from human action and is made possible by a universe of symbols.

3. Symbolism—whether verbal or otherwise—makes possible a self-created world of social reality and links the individual to a set of ongoing socially-constructed meanings.

4. Individuals interact in terms of such shared meanings and especially the meaning they attribute to each others' actions.

5. Social interaction may be viewed as a process of negotiation in which social valuables e.g., knowledge, status, etc., are exchanged and through which people express their self-identity.

These propositions are not equally accepted by all interactionist theorists and there are differences of opinion, centring around the last proposition. The 'action' perspective does, however, lead to a distinct kind of explanation of social phenomena and description of the social world.[6] Instead of grand theory and deductive categories we have grounded theory[7] and experiential categories. In general the 'action' perspective has a great deal of support as a type of approach and an explanation of social reality. But there are some criticisms too which should be noted:

(1) Explanation of social action tends to drift into theoretical anarchy—there is no attempt to make 'interpreted meaning' comparative or objective.

(2) All explanation is inherently abstractive—to deny this and claim that an action perspective embraces the 'real' meaning people give to their actions ignores the general abstractive role of theorizing.

(3) 'Action' categories are not logical categories and cannot, therefore, be used to construct scientifically adequate models.

(4) The stress on man as a social being neglects his links with the biological world of which he is a part and with which he interacts.

(5) It is ideologically motivated; the action model is conducive to radicalism and a stress on social change and political and social dissent.

[6] For a full discussion see P. L. Berger and T. Luckmann, *The Social Construction of Reality* (New York: Doubleday, 1966).

[7] B. G. Glaser and A. L. Strauss, *The Discovery of Grounded Theory* (Weidenfeld and Nicolson, 1968).

These criticisms may be defended and such a defence can be found elsewhere.[8] For immediate purposes the concern is how far these two general models of explanation—the functionalist systems approach originating in Durkheim and the social action approach formulated initially by Weber—link into different perspectives on organizations. The most fruitful way of answering such a question would be to identify the main exponents and see their contribution to the range of issues which have dominated organization theory.

Comparing organizations—social system and social action perspectives

Four basic questions have provided the focus of concern in the attempt to explore the nature and consequences of social organization:

(1) How far do organizations exist as identifiable entities, i.e. is it possible to distinguish their essential features?

(2) How far do such essential features enable the development of a comparative model which classifies different types of organizations?

(3) What relationships exist between the external contexts of organizations and their internal social, technological and political structures?

(4) In what ways do organizational features relate to the relationships and attitudes of those who comprise the membership of the organization?

These questions have been answered implicitly by social theorists who have been more concerned to develop an explanation linked to a general theoretical framework—or simply a problem-oriented approach—than a marriage of the two. It is open to judgment how far either the systems approach or the social action approach to organizations answers these questions.

System and goal models of organizations

The system approaches to defining and explaining organizations derive largely from the initial propositions of functionalism. Social organization in society is viewed as an outworking of general goals, different kinds of structures existing to cope with basic societal problems. The contribution of *Talcott Parsons* tends to be synonymous with this system orientation. Since his scheme has been used extensively to cope with a variety of theoretical and

[8] See especially A. M. Rose (ed.), *Human Behaviour and Social Processes* (Routledge, 1962).

organizational questions it illustrates initially what the system approach embodies.

Parsons claims that society can be defined by reference to four problems which have to be solved for society to survive and evolve. These problems are:

(1) Adaptation: accommodation to the reality of the demands of the environment coupled with the active transformation of the situation.

(2) Goal attainment: the definition of objectives and the mobilization of resources to attain them.

(3) Integration: establishing and organizing a set of relations among the member units that serve to co-ordinate and unify them.

(4) Latency: the maintenance over time of motivational and cultural patterns.

Smelser suggests that from the point of view of society as a whole certain sub-systems or institutions have the function of meeting these needs; the *economic* system of meeting adaptive needs, the *political* system of meeting goal attainment needs, *solidary groupings* such as the family or ethnic group of meeting integrative needs, and the *cultural* system of meeting the needs of latency. As Devereaux remarks, the fit between these basic system problems and institutions is far from perfect,[9] but Parsons would reply that such classification refers to the *primacy* of orientation only. However, even with that proviso it is clear that such classification attempts to identify organizations by the needs or goals they serve. And from this emerges the basic system view that the internal structure is shaped by the success in attaining such goals. For Parsons organizations may themselves be regarded as partly open systems, and as such they have to solve at a 'lower level' the four functional needs which are thought to characterize all social systems, i.e. organizations are societies 'writ small'. This isomorphic deductionism is a source of much of the confusion and tautology in Parsons' analysis, and those who have attempted to apply the scheme to particular problems and organizations have had some difficulty.

One writer who has adopted an approach similar to Parsons is *Argyris*, a neo-human relations theorist, who has suggested that the problem is not so much the total classification of organizations as an understanding of how the individual and the organization interact and influence each other.[10] Argyris suggests that formal

---

[9] In M. Black (ed.), *The Social Theories of Talcott Parsons* (Englewood Cliffs: Prentice Hall, 1961).

[10] C. Argyris, *Integrating the Individual and the Organization* (New York: Wiley, 1964).

organizations and individuals are basically organisms at different
levels of analysis and share five essential properties: (i) They
consist of a plurality of parts which (ii) maintain themselves
through their inter-relatedness and (iii) achieve specific objectives; whilst maintaining themselves and realizing particular
goals they (iv) adapt to their external environment and (v) thereby
maintain the inter-related state of parts.

From these five properties of organizations as organisms are
drawn several propositions. The parts of the organization cannot
be defined *a priori*—they may be individuals, groups or departments. Such parts are interdependent. All systems possess manifest
or latent goals which relate the organization to its environment.
Such a relationship makes the organization a partly open system.
This poses the difficult issue of where the organization ends and
the environment begins—an issue taken up by Katz and Kahn.[11]
Finally Argyris suggests that organizations as systems possess
three *core activities*: (i) achievement of objectives, (ii) internal
maintainance and (iii) external adaptation. This is not so different
from Parsons' system problems, but here the similarity ends.
Argyris suggests that the five system dimensions of organizations
can be used to define a polar type—the 'axiologically good
organization'. This kind of organization is good because it makes
for individual mental health.

Argyris recognizes that organizations have different societal
contexts and different histories and that how these influence the
organization is subject to research and empirical analysis.
However he maintains that 'in so far as the axiologically good
organization is consonant with individual mental health' it is so
because the latter is positively related to 'the capacity of the
individual to produce, to be committed, creative and flexible'
and these factors will 'enhance the organization's capacity to
achieve its goals, survive and grow', i.e. that in the last resort
organizations can only be successful by creating the conditions for
mentally healthy individuals.

Argyris leaves open the issue of whether the organization is a
totally open system. *Katz and Kahn* have no doubt; the organization is a completely open system, and the central question posed
is that of *boundary interchange*. The open system does not *a priori*
preclude feed-back processes, which may be essential for survival,
and which can broadly be analysed in terms of input, throughput
and output processes. All organizations contain elements which
fulfil productive, maintenance, adaptive and managerial-political

[11] D. Katz and R. Kahn, *The Social Psychology of Organizations* (New York:
Wiley, 1966).

functions. The analogy is with the biological model or the view that natural and social systems are similar. Such systems import energy and process it in a cyclical way. They contain life-renewing or 'negative entrophy' elements and maintain themselves in some kind of dynamic equilibrium or homeostasis. The parallel between natural and social systems, as Katz and Kahn recognize, is not totally adequate. Social systems have no distinct boundaries, are much more flexible internally and are produced through human choice rather than genetic accident. Individuals knit into such systems but only, in their view, by being regulated through the normative component of the roles they occupy. Katz and Kahn attribute to values the integrating function within the system, these in turn reflecting the values of the wider society. The system model they develop, like that of Parsons, contains particular assumptions which have been neatly summarized by Silverman:[12]

'The Systems approach stresses the way in which the action of the parts is structured by the system's need for stability and goal-consensus, and emphasises the processes of integration and adaptation . . . in assuming that organisations "exist as instruments for the attainment of valued future states", [the Systems approach] has limited itself . . . tending to play down the political and status concerns of those concerned and implying that goals and actions are largely conditioned by the problems of the organisation and by role-expectations as defined by the formal structure.'

The weakness of the system model of organizations is not shared by all theories which try to classify organizations according to their goals. The work of *Etzioni* avoids some of the worst excesses and tautology of the system analogy.[13] Etzioni uses the variable of *compliance* to develop a goal-based model which he regards as mainly relevant to the 'lower participants' of organizations. Compliance has both relational and psychological elements in that it refers both to 'a relation in which an actor behaves in accordance with a directive supported by another actor's power' and 'the orientation of the subordinated actor to the power applied'. Compliance, then, is the 'major element of the relationship between those who have power and those over whom they exercise it and is universal, existing in all social units'. In developing compliance as a basis for organization classification, Etzioni distinguishes three steps: (1) a distinction between three kinds of power, (2) a distinction between three kinds of involvement,

[12] D. Silverman, *The Theory of Organisations* (Heinemann, 1970), pp. 39–41.
[13] A. Etzioni, *A Comparative Analysis of Complex Organizations* (New York: Free Press, 1961).

(3) the association between kinds of power and kinds of involvement. It is 'these associations which are the compliance relationships and which serve as a basis for organization classification'.

Etzioni considers that power can best be identified through the means adopted by its holders to achieve any particular end. Thus while *coercive*, *remunerative* and *normative* means may be present in any one formal structure, he considers them sufficiently distinct to form three very different types. Each type is the basis of a particular attitude response or orientation by those to whom it is applied. An individual's involvement is the 'cathectic-evaluative orientation of an actor towards an object' and (1) coercive means tend to produce *alienative* involvement, (2) remunerative means tend to produce *calculative* involvement, and (3) normative means tend to produce *moral* involvement. This strain towards congruency between the relational and the psychological elements of compliance, Etzioni suggests, derives from 'internal and external pressures on the organization to be effective'. Effective for whom is not quite clear but this congruency tendency is used to identify organizations of three major kinds: those which use coercion as a basic method of control and produce alienative involvement; those which use remunerative methods and produce calculative involvement; and those which use normative methods, such as religious and voluntary organizations, and produce moral involvement. Etzioni, having linked the elements of compliance to different types of organization, suggests that, if it is possible to construct a goal model at all, then it derives from the effectiveness of the compliance relationships. Prisons and coercive organizations tend to be effective in terms of the goal of *order*; firms tend to be effective in terms of *economic goals*; religious and voluntary associations in terms of *cultural goals*. Etzioni is much more subtle than this sketch would suggest but he does leave in doubt several issues:

(1) Exactly what governs the degree to which individuals permit the compliance relationship of any one situation permanently to affect both how they view themselves and the roles they occupy?

(2) The influence of different kinds of compliance upon people occupying different positions within the same organization.

(3) The extent to which organizational factors—organization size, work or production technology in particular—influence the compliance process.

(4) The relationship between organizational diversity and the structural–functionalist view of social institutions.

Etzioni is not the only theorist to formulate a goal-oriented approach to organizational analysis which is not directly linked to the systems model of society. *Perrow* has recently tried to clarify some of the confusion surrounding the use of the concept of goals in organization theory.[14] He suggests that there are some basic objections which have yet to be resolved: that, strictly speaking, organizations do not have goals, only individuals do; that goals are difficult to observe and measure; and that any distinction between goals and means is difficult to make. His own solution is pragmatic and consists of listing 'five types or levels of goals . . . to deal with the question of whose point of view is being recognized, society, the customer, the investor, the top executive or others'.[15] These five types of goals are:

(1) *Societal goals* refer to society in general, e.g. to produce goods and services, maintain order and general cultural values.

(2) *Output goals* refer to the public in contact with the organization. 'This category deals with types of output defined in terms of consumer functions, e.g. consumer goods, education.'

(3) *System goals* refer to the state or manner of the functioning of the organization independent of the goods or services it produces or its derived goals, e.g. 'the emphasis upon growth, stability or upon modes of functioning such as being tightly or loosely controlled or structured'.

(4) *Product goals* refer to the characteristics of the goods or services produced, e.g. an 'emphasis upon quality or quantity, variety, availability, uniqueness'.

(5) *Derived goals* refer to the uses to which the organization puts the power it generates in pursuit of other goals, e.g. 'political aims, community services, employee development, investment and plant-location policies'.

Perrow is most concerned not to minimize the fundamental problems posed by talking of organizational goals. He recognizes that in relation to any one organization they may be multiple and also conflicting, and can be pursued all at once or in sequence; that such goals are problematical rather than given and obvious; and that, since organizations differ in their tasks, then they will differ in their structure or the way they are run. It is possible to conceptualize the structure of any kind of organization, Perrow suggests, by linking the kind of tasks pursued by the organization with the degree of discretion, power, and interdependence of organizational groups and the basis of their co-ordination. The *poly-centralized structure* typifies those organizations where discretion, power and interdependence is *high* and the basis of co-ordination occurs through feedback processes. This structure

[14] C. Perrow, *Organizational Analysis* (Tavistock, 1970).
[15] *Ibid.*, p. 134.

tends to emerge because the organization has to deal with *non-routine tasks*. It contrasts with its polar opposite, the *formal centralized structure* where the discretion, power and inter-dependence of groups is *low* and the basis of co-ordination is through advance planning. Perrow claims that this is because the organization has to deal with *routine tasks*. These two polar types are very similar to what Burns and Stalker mean by 'organic' and 'mechanistic' organizational structures.[16] Perrow's general assertion, then, is that whether tasks are routine or non-routine will directly influence the kind of authority structure and pro-duction technology and that this generally is the basis for funda-mental differences in organization structures of all kinds—not just work organizations.

One question arising from Perrow's analysis is the relationship of the organizational goals he defines to the elements of structure which he suggests characterize all organizations. He is most explicit on this point. 'Throughout we were concerned to convey the diversity of organizational life—there is no one goal, there is no one best strategy—and yet to indicate that diversity has a pattern . . . we were not successful in laying out [such] a clear pattern, nor did we attempt to link goals to structure and tech-nology. Such sophistication if possible at all, will take some time to achieve.'[17]

The action framework and interactionist approach

The major propositions of the social action perspective have already been spelt out earlier in this chapter. Until recently little attempt has been made to make explicit such a perspective. There may be several reasons for this slow development:
(1) The belief that organizational theory has developed as an implicit attempt to control and manipulate people to fit into organizations, i.e. that some kind of professional conspiracy has existed.
(2) That organization analysis is an extension of an explanation of general societal structures and processes, i.e. that it is integral to systems theory.
(3) That, *a priori*, an approach which starts from the premiss of 'understanding the framework of meaning of individual or typical people' cannot move beyond the interpersonal level of explana-tion.

Each of these arguments contains an element of truth. It is doubtful whether there has been a 'conspiracy' amongst organiza-

[16] T. Burns and G. M. Stalker, *The Management of Innovation* (Tavistock, 1961).
[17] Perrow, *op. cit.*, p. 181.

tion theorists. There may have been some reluctance to examine what were defined as irrelevant questions, and it is fairly clear that many of the major lines of research have been dictated by the need to understand organizations *as a means* of resolving organization pathologies or abstract theoretical issues. This does not amount to a conspiracy—in spite of systems explanation having an inherent conservative bias and management theory being imbued with self-justification. Happily, in both cases, any ideological underpinning is giving way to a sceptical and probing assessment of the assumptions which guide the analysis of organizations. The critical framework of action theory is part of this assessment.

The second argument is also partly true. The claim to develop general models and paradigms of society has been in the long tradition of organicism. However there are other models, particularly in the Marxian and Weberian tradition, which have received relatively little attention and development.[18] Perhaps the decline of the influence of the systems approach reflects the re-emergence of the Weberian tradition in sociology. And perhaps it also reflects the need for sociology to become both useful and sensitized to the political and social choices which have to be made in the development of industrial society.[19]

The third claim is also one of substance. Is it really possible to develop a framework based on an assessment of how others perceive the social world? Does the construct 'framework of meaning' really provide any basis for comparing the refracted social reality people experience? Existential and phenomenological theorists tend to the view that actions are unique to the actor and that the symbolic universe is an extension of that uniqueness. An individual constructs his own social reality and interprets the world through his own biography. We are all different and have different experiences. Explanation, according to this view, is redundant. The less radical position is that of symbolic interactionism,[20] which claims that insight and understanding can occur through some knowledge of the way symbols are generated and used in behaviour. People interact in terms of shared meanings and these provide the framework which makes possible the interpretation of social relationships. This second

[18] See for example the argument by D. Lockwood, 'Social Integration and System Integration', in G. K. Zollschan and W. Hirsch, *Explorations in Social Change* (Routledge, 1964).

[19] A. Gouldner, *The Coming Crisis of Western Sociology* (Heinemann, 1971).

[20] See A. M. Rose, *op. cit.*, also C. Gordon and K. Gergen, *The Self in Social Interaction*, vol. I (Wiley, 1968).

position appears the more tenable, if only because of the fact of interaction—people do share 'meanings' and these are consensual, although not necessarily *a priori* so.

The critique by action theorists of what passes for explanation in sociology and what constitutes a sound approach to organizational analysis tends to fuse into a persuasive and critical assessment:

'If society is socially constructed, then the logic behind some sociological investigations becomes highly questionable. For to relate one structural variable to another, for example organizational form and economic environment, may fail to take account of the orientations of the people involved and the meanings which they attach to "efficiency", "the economy" and so on. It is out of factors like these that action is generated: to pay insufficient attention to them can involve the sociologist in an empty determinism. . . .'[21] And again 'the Systems approach tends to regard behaviour as a reflection of the characteristics of a social system containing a series of impersonal processes which are external to actors and constrain them. In emphasizing that action derives from the meaning that men attach to their own and others acts, the Action frame of reference is constrained by the way in which man socially constructs his reality'.[22]

The Action approach to organizations, albeit still rather in an *ad hoc* and formative stage, would appear to depend upon the following propositions:

(1) That social organization originates in the aims and purposes of individuals and groups.

(2) That the patterns of expectations and types of authority which govern actors' relationships are linked to the wider social context through the knowledge and culture of the participants.

(3) That actors' orientations differ; they may bring dissimilar interests and expectations to organization membership and participation, i.e. they may be differentially involved.

(4) That sources of differential involvement may be inside or outside the organization.

(5) That organization roles or patterns of norms refer to sets of shared expectations which are open to negotiation and change.

(6) That organization change has both internal and external sources but can be analysed through patterns of expectations and attitude orientations.

There is nothing particularly new about these propositions and they have been implicit in the development and findings of a

[21] Silverman, *op. cit.*, p. 135.
[22] *Ibid.*, p. 141.

variety of work on organizations. Indeed it could be argued that an Action framework applied to organization theory has been slow to develop *because* it was there all the time. Such writers as Goffman, Sayles, Lupton, Dubin, Blauner, Goldthorpe—to name but a few—have focused on some particular issue or problem using one or more of these propositions. Some such contributions are dealt with in subsequent chapters of this section.

In short, the Action perspective is one in which the diversity and richness of human behaviour finds a place; it provides a balance—some would claim an alternative—to System models of explanation. Instead of *reified* processes and structural absolutes, the concern is with *experienced* processes and the perceived choices which underpin behaviour patterns. It is a more demanding perspective in the sense of not permitting vague and untestable generalizations; and maybe it is also more rewarding than the sterility of the Systems approach.

Conclusion

The reader may be forgiven for gaining the impression that organization theory is rather like a flying saucer—never seen in the same place twice. The range of issues is diverse and possible models, although clustering around the two major perspectives discussed, are different in their emphases. This leads to the sober conclusion that there are no grounds for complacency, least of all in the critical discussion of the ideas and findings reviewed. These ideas and findings assume particular importance in relation to the analysis of work organizations and are developed and assessed in the following chapters of this section.

CHAPTER 8

Human Relations and the Work Group

IN this chapter we shall examine the origins and development of the Human Relations movement and attempt to assess its contribution to industrial sociology and particularly to the study of work groups. This contribution has been varied and significant, but is nevertheless typically characterized by certain important limitations and has frequently been criticized. In recent years new and more adequate approaches to the study of work groups have been developed.

Early approaches to human behaviour at work

A proper understanding of the contribution of the Human Relations movement, and of its strengths and weaknesses, demands that some attention be given to earlier approaches to human behaviour at work. These were the background against which the Human Relations studies developed from the late 1920s onwards. The three most important of such approaches were perhaps those of classical economics, scientific management and early industrial psychology and physiology.[1]

Put oversimply, the assumptions economists made about the behaviour of individuals, as entrepreneurs or workers, included the following: that individuals acted in isolation and without regard for others; that they acted in pursuit of their own interests so as to maximize their income; and that they acted rationally, logically relating means and ends. This view was made notorious when Elton Mayo, the 'father' of the Human Relations movement, attacked it as the 'rabble hypothesis': 'Natural society consists of a horde of unorganized individuals; every individual acts in a manner calculated to secure his own self-preservation and self-

[1] See G. Friedmann, *Industrial Society* (Glencoe: Free Press, 1955).

interest; every individual thinks logically and to the best of his ability, in the service of this aim'.[2]

This sort of approach to human motivation and behaviour was also accepted by many others including the proponents of Scientific Management, whose work it underlies. F. W. Taylor and his associates attempted to apply scientific methods to industrial work. Their approach included the assumptions that men could be related to their work rather as machines to be made as efficient as possible; that, properly used, incentives would evoke more, and more efficient, work by the employee; and that the financial rewards from the increases in efficiency which would result from the use of Scientific Management could be used to increase the income of both managers and workers and thus secure the harmonious co-operation of both groups.

Taylor's ideas aroused a great deal of controversy and opposition even at the time. His assumptions about human behaviour were criticized in the light of findings regarding, for example, the effects of cumulative fatigue and the variations in abilities between workers. Such research stressed the importance of the 'human factor', and directed attention to environmental conditions—heating, lighting, colour, hours of work and rest pauses—and to their effects on workers' behaviour.

THE HAWTHORNE EXPERIMENTS

The Human Relations movement arose as a reaction against all these approaches with their individualistic and over-rational emphasis, and their tendencies to explain workers' behaviour as a response to their environment defined largely in material terms. The investigations at the Hawthorne Works of the Western Electric Company in Chicago between 1927 and 1932 have been widely reported.[3] They developed out of lighting experiments in the earlier tradition, the investigators being forced to take social factors increasingly into account to explain their results. The three main stages were a study of a small group of women workers in the Relay Assembly Test Room, attempting unsuccessfully to

---

[2] Elton Mayo, *The Social Problems of an Industrial Civilization* (Routledge, 1949), p. 37f.

[3] For the full account see F. J. Roethlisberger and W. J. Dickson, *Management and the Worker* (Cambridge, Mass.: Harvard University Press, 1939). For an excellent summary: H. A. Landsberger, *Hawthorne Revisited* (Ithaca, N.Y.: Cornell University Press, 1958), pp. 4–27.

relate output to hours of work and rest pauses; an extensive interviewing programme using increasingly non-directive methods;
and observation of a group of men in the Bank Wiring Observation
Room for a period of six months, revealing complex 'informal'
organization and group control over levels of output and other
forms of behaviour.

The historical importance of these studies is undoubted. They
demonstrated the practicality and value of empirical research in
industrial organizations. It could fairly be claimed as a result of
the experiments that the earlier approaches were shown to be
inadequate: 'many significant variations [in output] could not
be related to physical working conditions alone'; 'the efficiency
of a wage incentive was so dependent on its relation to other
factors that it was impossible to consider it as a thing in itself
having an independent effect on the individual'.[4] The worker
could no longer be regarded as a socially isolated individual who
acted rationally and independently of his fellows to maximize his
income. The existence of 'informal' organization had been 'discovered', and group influences on workers' behaviour and output
had been observed in great detail, though the varying nature of
such influences was less clearly accounted for. In addition, the
study outlined the beginnings of a model of the factory as a social
system, and of the worker as 'social man'.

The Hawthorne experiments have probably been more often
discussed than any other single piece of research in industrial
sociology. Landsberger has shown that much of the relevant
literature can best be regarded as criticism of the use made of the
research results, the ways in which they have been popularized,
and the general approach and philosophy of the Human Relations
'school', rather than as criticism of the Experiments themselves.
It is true that some of the methods used appear unsophisticated
in comparison with subsequent developments in this field, and
in particular studies of single specially selected small groups were
relied upon as the basis for far-reaching generalizations. Many
of the observations and results are capable of alternative interpretations to those given by the investigators: on the basis of a
detailed examination of the published data Carey claims that the
findings of the Relay Assembly Test Room studies could be used
to emphasize the importance of monetary incentives, driving
leadership and discipline; Blumberg argues that the key to understanding the same results is the growth of participation by the
workers; whilst Cubbon defends the original researchers' interpre-

[4] Roethlisberger and Dickson, *op. cit.*, pp. 160-1.

tations when they are seen in context.[5] Nevertheless the studies performed the important functions of showing that certain basic assumptions were inadequate and of directing subsequent research to a number of hitherto neglected factors.

We shall therefore consider first the directions taken by subsequent research in this tradition, and the general philosophical position taken up by Mayo in particular, before considering the criticisms which can be made of this approach to the analysis of industrial organizations.

RESEARCH ON HUMAN RELATIONS IN INDUSTRY

There is by now a considerable body of research in the Human Relations tradition. The main themes of much of this work can be traced back to problems raised by the Hawthorne experiments. Different perspectives from other sources have also been included and these themes have been developed in quite varied ways.

First, both the Relay Assembly Test Room and the Bank Wiring Observation Room demonstrated the importance of group influences on individual behaviour at work, though the analysis of why the former group co-operated so well with management and the latter obstructed management's goals was less satisfactory. In particular the Test Room results directed attention to the ways in which supervisors behaved and to communications between management and workers. Such lines of thought were strengthened by the work of Lewin and others experimenting with 'authoritarian', 'laissez faire' and 'democratic' styles of leadership in small groups, in which the most satisfied groups were those with democratic leadership.[6] The relationship of these variables— styles of leadership, productivity, morale and group participation in decision making—were tested in a number of experimental and quasi-experimental studies.

Well known and typical examples of such studies include the experiment in a clothing factory in which Coch and French found that groups allowed to participate in planning changes of work showed less resistance to the change, higher levels of output achieved more quickly after the change, and less dissatisfaction

[5] A. Carey, 'The Hawthorne Studies: a Radical Criticism', *American Sociological Review*, 1967, 32, pp. 403-16; P. Blumberg, *Industrial Democracy* (Constable, 1968); A. Cubbon, 'Hawthorne Talk in Context', *Occupational Psychology*, 1969, 43, pp. 111-28.

[6] See for example R. White and R. Lippitt, 'Leader Behaviour and Member Reaction in Three "Social Climates"' in D. Cartwright and A. Zander (eds.), *Group Dynamics* (Tavistock, 1953), pp. 585-611.

than groups which had not been allowed to participate in this way.[7]
This and many other studies[8] appeared to reinforce some of the
possible interpretations of the Hawthorne Experiments, but
further research has been less conclusive. For example, some
workers allowed to participate in making decisions have tried to
expand the scope for them and have come up against management's
refusal to delegate more authority.[9] In a replication of the Coch
and French experiment in a Norwegian factory the investigators
found that there were no significant differences in production
as a result of participation in decision making.[10] The inadequacy
of a narrowly based social-psychological framework for enquiry
has been increasingly apparent, and more recently both critics
and proponents of this type of research have stressed the need to
consider explicitly the broader organizational and social setting.[11]

A second group of studies has been concerned with continuing
the analysis of the structure and functioning of small groups in
industry, extending this to the whole organization and developing
an analytical framework for this purpose around the study of
'interaction'. For example, Homans, using the basic concepts of
'action', 'interaction' and 'sentiments', reanalysed the Bank
Wiring Observation Room data, and by comparing it with other
small group studies developed general propositions about small
groups.[12] Whyte, in a large number of studies in industry, and
using a fairly similar approach, has explored problems which
have been neglected by many Human Relations researchers. These
include union–management relations and the different patterns
of interaction which developed as the pattern of industrial relations
changed towards 'industrial peace'; the effect of type of work flow
and of changes in technology on interaction and sentiments within
groups and organizations; and the consequences of the use of

[7] L. Coch and J. R. P. French, Jun., 'Overcoming Resistance to Change', Human
Relations, 1948, pp. 512–32.

[8] For example D. Katz et al., Productivity, Supervision and Morale among Railroad
Workers (Ann Arbor, Mich.: Survey Research Centre, 1951); D. Katz et al.,
Productivity, Supervision and Morale in an Office Situation, Part 1 (Survey Research
Center, 1951); or see R. L. Kahn and D. Katz, 'Leadership Practices in Relation
to Productivity and Morale', in Cartwright and Zander, op. cit., pp. 612–28.

[9] H. L. Wilensky, 'Human Relations in the Workplace', in C. M. Arensberg
et al., Research in Industrial Human Relations (New York: Harper 1957), pp. 25–50;
M. Bucklow, 'A New Role for the Work Group', Administrative Science Quarterly,
1966, pp. 59–78.

[10] J. R. P. French, Jun., J. Israel and D. As, 'An Experiment on Participation in
a Norwegian Factory', Human Relations, 1960, 13, pp. 3–19.

[11] See for example Wilensky, op. cit.; E. H. Schein, Organizational Psychology
(Englewood Cliffs, N.J.: Prentice Hall, 1965).

[12] G. C. Homans, The Human Group (Routledge, 1951).

incentive payment systems on individual, group and plant-wide bases.[13] Other leading 'interactionists' have claimed that this approach provides a dynamic analysis which makes it possible to predict and to come to grips with the movement of a social system.[14]

Thirdly, Lloyd Warner and his associates have extended Human Relations research in another direction to take account of environmental factors. In the course of a major study of a New England community, referred to as Yankee City, they analysed the place of industrial organizations in the local community and the ways in which they may be affected by wider economic and social changes. Thus their explanation of a strike was in terms of 'internal' and 'external' factors: there had been changes in the technology, occupational structure and skill hierarchy within the factory, the development of mass markets and absentee ownership, and a change in the status of factory management in the local community.[15]

THE INFLUENCE OF ELTON MAYO

The Hawthorne experiments were first popularized by Elton Mayo and his interpretation of their significance and that of a small number of other studies of working groups has had a very wide influence.[16] Mayo was alarmed by the social disorganization and conflict which he saw as deriving from the breakdown of the 'established' society of the pre-industrial period. Man's scientific and technical discoveries had led to the break-up of this established society but his knowledge of social processes was inadequate for the creation of an 'adaptive' society. Mayo saw the solution to the problem of anomie in the modern world in the development of social skills, particularly by managers and administrators, and the maintenance by them of the 'spontaneous co-operation' in industry which the Hawthorne experiments and other research had shown was possible. Within industrial organizations in cohesive small work groups, men could find the sense of belonging and the social purpose which they had lost. He saw conflict as pathological; it

[13] W. F. Whyte, *Pattern for Industrial Peace* (New York: Harper, 1951); *Money and Motivation* (New York, Harper, 1955); *Men at Work* (Homewood, Ill.: Dorsey Press, 1961).
[14] C. M. Arensberg and G. Tootell, 'Plant Sociology: Real Discoveries and New Problems', in M. Komarovsky (ed.), *Common Frontiers of the Social Sciences* (Glencoe: Free Press, 1957), pp. 310–37.
[15] W. L. Warner and J. O. Low, *The Social System of the Modern Factory* (New Haven: Yale University Press, 1947).
[16] E. Mayo, *The Human Problems of an Industrial Civilization* (New York: Macmillan, 1933); and *op cit.*

could and must be resolved by developing a sense of shared purpose within industrial organizations and the realization that social satisfactions as well as material rewards were of importance to the worker.

These ideas have not only provided an underlying philosophy for much research in industry, but they have also influenced managerial practice, and perhaps even more, managerial ideologies, as Bendix and others have pointed out.[17] In Britain and the United States especially much Human Relations training has been undertaken, particularly of supervisors, though experimental and other studies have generally failed to demonstrate that such training achieves the desired results.[18] The limitations of training based on Human Relations ideas, and the ambiguity of many of the results of research designed to test Human Relations propositions, have added to the growing body of criticism of this tradition of investigation.

LIMITATIONS OF THE HUMAN RELATIONS TRADITION

Human Relations, narrowly conceived as merely the Hawthorne experiments or the work of Mayo, or so all embracing that it includes almost everybody who ever mentions 'human relations in industry', has been subjected to recurrent barrages of criticism over the last twenty-five years. As will be obvious from the references made so far, not all points of criticism are equally applicable, or indeed applicable at all, to all the investigations within this tradition. With this reservation in mind, however, it is possible to try to summarize the criticisms which have been made and to see why more recent studies of work groups have taken a rather different direction.

The most obvious target for criticism has been Mayo's sweeping analysis of the problems of industrial societies. This has been attacked as involving a misinterpretation of the past, of the nature of pre-industrial society, and more important as seeing only one of the many possible solutions to the problems of the present.[19]

[17] R. Bendix, *Work and Authority in Industry* (New York: Wiley, 1956); L. Baritz, *The Servants of Power* (New York: Wiley, 1960); J. Child, *British Management Thought* (Allen & Unwin, 1969).

[18] J. H. Goldthorpe, 'La conception des conflits du travail dans l'enseignement des relations humaines', *Sociologie du Travail*, 1961, pp. 1–17; E. F. Harris and E. Fleishman, 'Human Relations and the Stability of Leadership Patterns', *Journal of Applied Psychology*, 1955, pp. 20–5.

[19] See for example H. L. Sheppard, 'Approaches to Conflict in American Industrial Sociology', *British Journal of Sociology*, 1954, pp. 324–41; C. Kerr and L. Fisher, 'Plant Sociology: the Elite and the Aborigines', in M. Komarovsky (ed.), *op. cit.*

Many of the factory workers studied by Mayo and his colleagues were first or second generation immigrants living in rapidly growing and changing urban areas, and their 'anomie' cannot be seen as a necessarily permanent feature of industrial societies. Even if this analysis were correct, Mayo ignores the possibilities of building social integration and belongingness through associations such as churches, communities and trade unions rather than the factory and the work group within it. In his writings research on small groups is applied to the analysis of whole societies without any apparent awareness of the different problems and levels of explanation involved.

Much writing in the Human Relations tradition is not concerned with such problems, but nevertheless suffers from limitations which are not unconnected with the weakness of the Mayo perspective. The most central of these limitations is in the analysis of the causes and nature of industrial conflict. Human Relations research, from the Hawthorne experiments onwards, has successfully shown how interpersonal and intergroup conflicts within industry can arise from the ineffective communications and 'bad' supervisory or management practices. They have appeared less aware of the limitations of such an analysis and of the existence of conflicts of interest between groups which derive from their positions in the structure of industrial organizations and industrial societies.[20] The emphasis on the social satisfactions to be gained from membership of a cohesive work group has distracted attention from the question of economic rewards, from the conflict of interests over the distribution of the income of the enterprise as wages or profits, and the power differential between management and workers. Mayo's concern for harmony in the wider society has been paralleled by a concern with co-operation and equilibrium within the factory, and a failure, on the whole, to see the functions of conflict, its inescapability in a 'free' society, and to see 'that it is precisely the freedom to conflict which establishes the boundaries within which the actual conflicts can be contained'.[21] Analysis has centred on the integrating rather than the differentiating factors within the plant, and as such has been one-sided.[22]

[20] H. L. Sheppard, op. cit., and 'The Treatment of Unionism in "Managerial Sociology"', American Sociological Review, 1949, pp. 310–13; R. C. Sorenson, 'The Concept of Conflict in Industrial Sociology', Social Forces, 1951, pp. 263–7. The Bank Wiring Room study is only a partial exception to this point.

[21] R. Bendix and L. Fisher, 'The Perspectives of Elton Mayo', in A. Etzioni (ed.), Complex Organizations (New York: Holt, Rinehart, 1961), pp. 113–26.

[22] G. Friedmann, 'Philosophy Underlying the Hawthorne Investigations', Social Forces, 1949, pp. 204–9, and op. cit., pp. 315–25.

Many of the other criticisms which can be made are related to this fundamental one. Thus, with some exceptions, (such as Whyte's and Warner's work referred to above), trade unions and industrial relations have been largely ignored in Human Relations research. Unions did not exist in the Hawthorne works in 1927 —though it has been claimed that at that time and later the Company spent considerable sums to prevent their organization;[23] but subsequent research cannot always make that claim. They have been difficult to accommodate within the Human Relations approach, except perhaps as associations oriented to management goals, and there has been no clear examination or understanding of their origin, functions or essential nature. Similarly, analysis of industrial relations has tended to remain within the plant, or even be limited to face-to-face relations. It is difficult to explain within a Human Relations frame of reference why certain industries should have consistently high and others consistently low strike records;[24] a monopoly of Human Relations skills by those in certain industries seems improbable, but broader social and economic factors have rarely been considered.

A further and often justified criticism of Human Relations research is that it 'stops at the plant gates'. The relationship of internal and external influences on an individual's behaviour at work is discussed in considerable detail in *Management and the Worker*, and Warner's study was explicitly concerned with industry-community relations. However, much research, most notably that in the social-psychological tradition, has considered work groups and worker-supervisor relations in isolation from the wider organizational and social setting. Even where the organizational setting has been seen to be important, there has rarely been recognition of the economic and social forces outside the plant which constrain management and workers' behaviour within it. The influence of the depression on the Hawthorne experiments was noted but neither at the time, nor later, were the implications for the understanding of organizational behaviour fully worked out. Human Relations research has tended to be unsatisfactory in just the areas which require explicit and systematic consideration of extra-organizational factors.

These limitations of the Human Relations approach have been ascribed to failure by the investigators to recognize and make explicit their own value orientations, their preferences for col-

[23] Landsberger, *op. cit.*, pp. 51–2.
[24] C. Kerr and A. J. Siegel, 'The Inter-Industry Propensity to Strike', in A. Kornhauser *et al.* (eds), *Industrial Conflict* (New York: McGraw-Hill, 1954), pp. 188–212.

laboration and stability in society rather than conflict and change.[25] Furthermore, this bias is linked to an acceptance of management's definition of the goals of the enterprise; the divergent and conflicting values of groups in industrial societies have not been recognized.[26] This is related to both the choice of problems for research (neglect of unions and industrial relations, for example) and the implications of research for managerial practice. Defenders of Human Relations research can justifiably point to the importance of its contribution to social scientific knowledge and understanding, but it is undeniable that intentionally or not much of the research, because of the value orientations of the researchers, has served to increase management's control over workers. The most notorious example of this is perhaps the personnel counselling programme at the Hawthorne works, which was introduced in the light of the success—as a means of releasing tension—of the non-directive interviewing during the experiments. The Wilenskys claim that 'counselling has helped protect management's freedom to promote, downgrade, transfer, train, discipline, lay off, apply a variety of rewards and sanctions (with a minimum of interference from a relatively co-operative union)— in short it has helped the company retain its control over the worker'.[27]

Secondly, the limitations of the Human Relations analysis of industrial enterprises can be related to basic theoretical and methodological weaknesses. Much of the research has been empirical, with few theoretical developments and limited use of the theories and concepts of others. In particular, levels of analysis and explanation have not been clearly distinguished. Human Relations studies have been particularly concerned with interpersonal relations in small groups. The enterprise has been conceptualized, and in a limited way analysed, as a social system, but on the whole the organizational and institutional levels of analysis have been neglected. Yet an adequate explanation of behaviour in work groups demands an awareness of the influence of organizational and institutional factors; otherwise particular findings will be generalized without regard to context. Conversely it is not possible to assume that, for example, face-to-face relations

[25] Bendix and Fisher, op. cit.; W. A. Koivisto, 'Value, Theory and Fact in Industrial Sociology', American Journal of Sociology, 1953, pp. 564–72; Kerr and Fisher, op. cit.

[26] W. E. Moore, 'Current Issues in Industrial Sociology', American Sociological Review, 1947, pp. 651–7; Koivisto, op. cit.

[27] J. L. and H. L. Wilensky, 'Personal Counselling: The Hawthorne Case', American Journal of Sociology, 1951, pp. 265–80.

between workers and an individual manager or supervisor are necessarily paralleled by, or influenced by the same factors as, worker–management relations, or even more so, union–management relations at the level of the organization or of the total society. Yet all this often seems to be implicit in the Human Relations approach.

LATER 'HUMAN RELATIONS' APPROACHES

In recent years research in this tradition has taken rather different directions, so that those involved have been labelled as exponents of 'neo-human-relations'.[28] The new developments have been the result of both attempts to take account of the criticisms outlined above and the assimilation of ideas from other sources. For example, although the concept of the factory as a social system is discussed in *Management and the Worker*, recent developments of this approach in the Human Relations tradition have been able to draw on the by now considerable literature on the analysis of industrial organizations as systems (see Chapter 7).

The Hawthorne experiments were taken to provide evidence of the need to think in terms of 'social man'. Awareness of the nature of men's 'needs' has led to discussion of 'self-actualizing man' or 'complex man' rather than 'social man'.[29] It has been suggested that needs can be classified in a hierarchy ranging from simple needs for survival, safety and security to self-actualization needs in the sense of a man making maximum use of all his resources; and that meeting such needs to provide job satisfaction may involve both good 'hygiene' (removing factors like poor working conditions which lead to dissatisfaction) and providing motivating factors (e.g. recognition and achievement which fulfill the needs for esteem and self-actualization).[30] The awareness that modern industrial organizations were often structured so that they were unable to meet these 'needs' has led to the advocacy of alternative managerial philosophies and forms of organization.[31]

---

[28] J. H. Goldthorpe et al., *The Affluent Worker : Industrial Attitudes and Behaviour* (Cambridge University Press, 1968), p. 178.

[29] E. H. Schein, *op. cit.*, pp. 47–63.

[30] A. Maslow, *Motivation and Personality* (New York: Harper, 1964); F. Herzberg et al., *The Motivation to Work* (New York: Wiley, 1959); but see also T. D. Wall and G. M. Stephenson, 'Herzberg's Two-Factor Theory of Job Attitudes', *Industrial Relations Journal*, December 1970.

[31] C. Argyris, *Personality and Organization* (New York: Harper, 1957); D. McGregor, *The Human Side of Enterprise* (New York: McGraw-Hill, 1960).

There is no doubt that this work by organizational psychologists is considerably more sophisticated, theoretically and methodologically, than many of the pioneering efforts in the Human Relations tradition. Thus there is a strong awareness of the psychologically 'alienating' nature of many jobs in modern large scale organizations, due to the nature of their technology, division of labour and social organization. Two main points of criticism, however, can still be made. In the first place, the concept of the enterprise remains basically a unitary one in which the inherent conflicts of interest of employer and employee are not fully acknowledged, so that it is assumed that it should be possible to satisfy all employees' 'needs' without loss of organizational effectiveness, or indeed that the former is a necessary condition of the latter. Secondly, as Goldthorpe and colleagues have stressed, one cannot proceed from a general specification of individual human needs to the wants and expectations of particular individuals; '. . . wants and expectations are culturally determined *variables*, not psychological constants', so that 'analysis will more usefully begin with the orientations to work which are found to prevail, rather than with quite general assumptions about the needs which all workers have'.[32]

RECENT STUDIES OF WORK GROUPS

As a result of more recent research it is now possible to suggest approaches to the study of work groups which are more comprehensive and more adequate than most of those undertaken in the Human Relations tradition.

It is important, first of all, to distinguish between occupational categories, task groups and sociable groupings in industry. This has not always been done, yet the differences between them, the degree to which they exist at all in any industrial enterprise, and, where they do, the degree to which their memberships overlap, are of crucial importance. By occupational category we mean those with the same occupation (labourers, clerks, skilled fitters and so on), who may, but need not, form task groups—those, of the same or several occupations, who actually work together. Workers from the same occupational category and/or task group may also form sociable groupings (the 'informal' groups of the Human Relations tradition), or such groups may form independently along the lines of age, ethnic, religious or some other differences. Thus in the shipbuilding industry, for example, men in the same

---

[32] J. H. Goldthorpe *et al.*, *op. cit.*, pp. 178-9.

'trade' generally have a strong sense of common identity, though they may work in small 'task groups' with men with other skills; and the membership of task groups may change fairly rapidly to meet production demands, being much less stable than the men's 'informal' sociable groupings.[33]

Secondly, it is important to recognize that we cannot assume, as the Human Relations tradition tended to do, that industry is composed of primary groups with solidary relations between their members. A substantial number of workers are relatively isolated on the job, and, more important, for many workers work is not a 'central life interest' so that, although they may be on good terms with their mates, they do not regard them as friends nor have any real 'affective involvement' with them.[34] Similarly, workers in the same occupation and work situation do not always develop a sense of common identity and willingness to take collective action,[35] although this may emerge over time or with a change in circumstances. Timperley, for example, was able to observe the general hands at a new airport (comprising a number of different task groups) as a definite internal organization emerged. This enabled the men to develop a procedure for dealing with tips (which only some of them received), to organize social activities for themselves and their families, and to take collective action through representatives in defence of their interests in economic rewards and in equality and fairness, vis-à-vis management and the trade union. Timperley suggests that this autonomous development was facilitated by the physical location and work organization of the general hands, by the non-intervention of the union, and by the problem the men faced in trying to secure higher wages during a pay freeze.[36]

This study lends support to a third point, that groups of all three sorts must be seen as at least potentially active, attempting to structure the situation in terms of their own interests, and not merely the passive recipients of management initiatives. Indeed, one important problem is to explain how and why groups take action. This has been attempted by Sayles, for example, who has categorized work groups primarily in terms of their behaviour

[33] R. K. Brown et al., 'Leisure in Work: the occupational culture of shipbuilding workers', in M. A. Smith et al. (eds.), Society and Leisure in Britain (forthcoming).

[34] J. H. Goldthorpe et al., op. cit., pp. 45-63; see also A. Etzioni, A Comparative Analysis of Complex Organisations (New York: Free Press, 1961), pp. 165-6.

[35] See for example A. J. M. Sykes, 'Navvies: their Social Relations', Sociology, 3, 1969, pp. 157-72.

[36] S. R. Timperley, 'A Study of a Self-Governing Work Group', Sociological Review, 18, 1970, pp. 259-81.

—the methods they evolve to solve their day-to-day problems, their response to management and supervision, and the type of people they recognize as leaders.[37] On the basis of interviews and other data relating to 300 task and/or occupational groups in 30 plants in a variety of industries in the United States he distinguished four types. In each case the behaviour remained characteristic of the group over a period of time even when personnel changed.

'Apathetic' groups (e.g. many unskilled workers) had low levels of grievance activity, no clear leadership and little internal unity; they were not ranked as very co-operative or as high producers by management, and played little part in union affairs. The rather more united 'erratic' groups (e.g. automobile assembly line workers) were easily aroused into grievance activity but of a poorly controlled sort, inconsistent in terms of their own apparent goals; leadership was often highly centralized, and such groups, ranked as unsatisfactory employees by management, played an active part in the union especially in the organizational stages. With the highest level of grievance activity, 'strategic' groups (e.g. key groups such as welders) continuously, consistently and rationally used pressure in support of their interests; with a very high degree of internal unity, they participated strongly in union activities, supplying much of the leadership, but also had good records as employees with management. The most stable groups were the 'conservative' ones (e.g. garment cutters and toolroom personnel); highly united internally and ranked as the most satisfactory employees by management, they used restrained pressure to redress specific grievances and were generally less active in union affairs.

The explanation of these differences was sought in the ways in which social relations were affected by the technology and division of labour within a plant. The level of grievance activity appeared to be related primarily to the status of the work group in relation to other groups in a plant—those in the middle ranges were the most active; and the type of pressure exerted appeared to be related to the internal organization of the group—activities were well planned and controlled in groups with independent operations.

Sayles's analysis, which also included accounts of changes of behaviour over time, demonstrates how differences in behaviour can be related to the social structure and system of production of a plant, so that behaviour is seen in its organizational context.

[37] L. R. Sayles, *Behaviour of Industrial Work Groups* (New York: Wiley, 1958).

There was no assumption of harmony of interests between management and workers. Groups were seen as pursuing their common economic interests and seeking to change the situation to secure their interests in contrast to the 'informal' groups to which the Human Relations researchers drew attention as a source of social satisfaction and stability for the workers. It is doubtful whether these four types of groups will be found in all situations, or exhaust the range of possibilities; however, in studies in the coal industry and in shipbuilding the importance has been demonstrated of the social relations within different occupational groups and their position in the occupational hierarchy for their industrial relations behaviour.[38]

In a study of two workshops by means of participant observation Lupton was forced to consider not only the organizational context but also factors external to the factories concerned in order to explain the behaviour of work groups.[39] In both workshops workers were paid on an incentive scheme, but whereas in one case, a workshop assembling small transformers, the workers did not respond as intended by management but used an elaborate 'fiddle' to stabilize their earnings and effort, in the other, a waterproof garment factory, no such collective regulation of output occurred. The difference was not due to any superiority of one incentive scheme over the other from the workers' point of view, or to any differences in social satisfactions or in leadership skills or efficiency on the part of management and supervision.

The explanation lay, Lupton argued, partly in the differences which were 'internal' to the work situation, which contributed to the lack of a 'will to control' on the part of the garment workers. In their workshop the productive system was characterized by a minute breakdown of operations and a short time span, and the method of wage payment was straight piecework with no complex system of allowances providing opportunity for a 'fiddle'. Sociable groupings did not coincide with task groups and no collective attitude to output and earnings developed, the predominant attitude being 'looking after number one'. However, these factors, none of which were found in the other workshop studied, were related to the social and economic environment of the workshop. The industry consisted of small firms in an unstable and highly competitive market; seasonal unemployment was common; labour costs were a relatively high proportion of total

[38] W. H. Scott et al., Coal and Conflict (Liverpool: University Press, 1963); R. K. Brown et al., 'The Contours of Solidarity: social stratification and industrial relations in shipbuilding', British Journal of Industrial Relations, 9, 1972.
[39] T. Lupton, On the Shop Floor (Oxford: Pergamon, 1963).

costs; the trade union was weak, especially at workshop level. There was no opportunity for an 'indulgency pattern' such as characterized the other workshop with its completely different environment.

Given these differences of environment, social relations and production systems within the workshops, the behaviour of the respective groups of workers appeared to Lupton to represent a realistic appraisal of their interests in the light of the knowledge available to them. In contrast to the analysis of the Bank Wiring Observation Room data there was no implication that the behaviour was only to be explained in terms of a 'logic of sentiments'.

In a study of a workshop in the same waterproof garment industry, where production was differently organized but the same norm of 'militant competitive individualism' in the face of a stringent incentive payment scheme could be observed, Cunnison has also emphasized the importance of going beyond the factory itself for a satisfactory explanation. Indeed she suggests that the 'internal/external' dichotomy is not really viable and workers must be seen as playing a number of roles in overlapping systems of roles and as sharing certain values derived from the community from which they came.[40]

Although formulations differ in important ways, these more recent studies share a common emphasis on the importance of factors outside the group and indeed outside the organization altogether for the explanation of work group behaviour. Such approaches have stimulated systematic and comparative investigation of such 'contextual' factors and their interrelations.[41] Many of these studies have also given an important place in their explanations to the relationship of technology and social relations, which we consider in more detail in the next chapter.

[40] S. Cunnison, *Wages and Work Allocation* (Tavistock, 1966).
[41] See for example D. S. Pugh *et al.*, 'A Conceptual Scheme for Organizational Analysis', *Administrative Science Quarterly*, 8, 1963, pp. 289–315; and 'The Context of Organizational Structure', *Administrative Science Quarterly*, 14, 1969, pp. 91–114.

CHAPTER 9

Technology, Technical Change and Automation

THE relationship between technology and social structure in industry, between the productive process and the social relations which surround it, has been an important theme in the sociological analysis of industrial organizations, and indeed of industrial societies. This focus of interest is particularly emphasized in the parallel concern with the social consequences of technical innovations. In this chapter we shall examine some of the attempts which have been made to categorize types of production system and to relate aspects of the social structure of the enterprise to these types. This 'technological implications' approach, as it has been called, has been subject to criticism on both empirical and theoretical grounds. Although these criticisms do limit the importance of technology as a constraint on social relations in industry, changes in technology commonly have a considerable impact on social relations and the reactions of those subject to them have frequently been studied, particularly in cases where 'automation' is being introduced.

One of the difficulties in this field is that terms are very often used in vaguely defined ways. 'Technology' can be seen as referring to the particular machines and equipment employed in production, to the nature of the raw materials worked on and to the body of knowledge and ideas which makes possible the employment of such machines and equipment. It is important to bear in mind too that technology is itself a social product and not something separate with an autonomous development.

TECHNOLOGY AND SOCIAL STRUCTURE IN INDUSTRY

Living as they did during periods of rapid industrialization and technical change, many of the 'classical' sociologists were concerned with the problems of the relationship of technology and social structure. Thus, for example, in Marx's analysis of the development of human society a vital part was played by 'the change and development of the material means of production, of the forces of production'. 'The mode of production of material life conditions the social, political and intellectual life process in general.'[1] As another example, Durkheim's study of *The Division of Labour in Society* includes a highly perceptive account of the social consequences of the use of certain types of production system in what he terms 'abnormal forms' of the division of labour.[2] More recently writers such as Friedmann have explored the consequences of developments in industry, in part caused by technological changes, which lead among other things to extreme specialization and fragmentation of tasks.[3]

Though such approaches provided illuminating overall views of developments in modern industrial societies, they were too general to encompass adequately the great variety of situations which more detailed research revealed. In recent years various attempts have been made to distinguish different types of production system and to identify the social characteristics which appear to be associated with each of them. Such attempts were confined initially to manufacturing industry, and independently produced remarkably similar conclusions; in the last few years the same approach has been extended to other sorts of organizations.

Woodward has explored the possibility of distinguishing between unit and small batch production, large batch and mass production, and process production. Her scheme, which in its fullest form comprises nine stages and two mixed types, is based on differences in technical complexity and the degree to which it is possible to exercise control over manufacturing operations and to reduce areas of uncertainty.[4] She pointed out that these types form stages in the chronological development of industry towards increasing standardization of products and increasing mechanization. This view is also shared by Touraine and Blauner, whose work is discussed below. However, it is not to be taken to mean that the development is in any sense inevitable or unilinear, or that a firm using process production methods is necessarily

---

[1] K. Marx and F. Engels, *Selected Works*, vol. I (Moscow: Foreign Languages Publishing House, 1958), pp. 90, 363.

[2] E. Durkheim, *The Division of Labour in Society* (Glencoe: Free Press, 1933), especially Book 3.

[3] G. Friedmann, *The Anatomy of Work* (Heinemann, 1961).

[4] J. Woodward, *Industrial Organization* (Oxford University Press, 1965); and *Management and Technology*, Problems of Progress in Industry, No. 3 (HMSO, 1958).

'progressive' or a firm making varied products in small quantities is in any sense 'backward'. The appropriate production system depends on the objectives of the enterprise.

A French sociologist, Touraine, also distinguishes three main stages in the development of technology and sees them as arising from the interaction of two contrasting processes. On the one hand there is a disintegration of the worker's skill; the work previously performed by one man is broken down into its component parts. On the other hand such a process makes possible the mechanization of these tasks and the development of an integrated production process which is in a sense automatic. Thus one moves from the old system of work based on craft skills using universal or flexible machines to produce a diversity of products, through a transitional stage characterized by unskilled workers feeding machines or performing very few simple operations to produce standardized products, to automation where the worker superintends, records and controls rather than does direct productive work.[5]

The third writer, Blauner, outlines four types of technology which arise from the long-run trend to increasing mechanization and increasing standardization of the product. 'Craft' industries, such as printing, he argues, have no standardized product, and therefore no possibility for extreme rationalization and standardization, but are dependent on the skills of the craftsman. 'Machine minding' industries, such as textiles, show a considerable degree of standardization and mechanization with the worker feeding and supervising the machine. 'Assembly line' industries, such as the automobile industry, are based on extreme fragmentation of work and rationalization of production of standardized products. It is here, he claims, that the problem of 'alienation' is most acute. 'Process' industries, such as chemicals, are the most highly mechanized, producing a uniform product in a continuous process.[6]

Each of the authors emphasizes certain reservations. Thus, though most industrial enterprizes can be typified as having one or another type of technology, not all tasks in the organization will be similar to those typical of that type of production process (e.g. maintenance work in all types of industry involves craft skills) and some organizations may be difficult to categorize. None of the writers suggests that social relations are technologically

[5] A. Touraine, 'An Historical Theory in the Evolution of Industrial Skills', in C. R. Walker (ed.), *Modern Technology and Civilization* (New York: McGraw-Hill, 1962), pp. 426–37.

[6] R. Blauner, *Alienation and Freedom* (Chicago: University Press, 1964).

determined; rather technology sets limits within which, for example, management policies operate, and there is scope for different allocations of the tasks to be done. The scope for choice may itself vary with technology—Woodward, for example, suggests that it is greatest in large-batch production situations. The economic structure of the industry may also lead to important differences, as may the character and expectations of the labour force.

In general, however, it is suggested that the two extremes of the technological scale are in many respects more similar to each other than to large batch and mass production systems. Thus, the meaninglessness of the worker's tasks and his powerlessness are seen as greatest on the assembly line. In the 'craft' industry the worker has considerable autonomy, which may, as in printing, be reinforced by strong trade union organization, and he can see the relevance of his contribution to the final product. In process production the operative needs to understand the nature of a substantial part of the production system to carry out his task, which involves considerable responsibility. At the same time he may be able to vary the sequence of operations, and except in crisis situations he does not work under great pressure, output being determined by the capacity of the plant rather than the worker's effort.

Influences on social relations on the shop floor are complex and varied (see Chapter 8). However, Sayles' work illustrates that knowledge of the place of work groups in the production system may be very important for the understanding of differences in their behaviour.[7] At a more general level it is argued that here too there are similarities between the two ends of the technological scale. In 'craft' industries workers may not be functionally interdependent but share common craft identity and membership of an occupational community with some or all of their fellow employees. Because of a certain freedom of movement on the job they also have opportunity for the growth of social relations with other workers. At the other end of the scale process technology commonly demands teamwork from small internally structured work groups which can be a source of social satisfaction and make for a highly cohesive organization. 'Machine-minding' and 'assembly line' technologies, in contrast, tend to tie the worker physically to the machine or place on the line and yet also leave him without membership of a clearly defined work group.

Management–worker relations are influenced by many factors other than technology, but it has been suggested that in this

[7] L. R. Sayles, *Behaviour of Industrial Work Groups* (New York: Wiley, 1958).

respect too the large batch/mass production systems, because of the nature of the situational demands of the production processes, give rise to more intense conflict than the two ends of the scale. It is in these situations that the pressures on the worker to maximize output tend to be greatest. With less standardized products, less complex technology, and more highly skilled workers it may be accepted that workers are unlikely to work well 'with a gun at their backs'; and with process production there is generally less pressure and the plant itself can contribute 'a framework of discipline and control' which may be less resented than authority exercised by a superior.[8]

Woodward's survey also revealed that management structure was related to plant technology. Certain characteristics (for example, the length of the line of command and the ratio of managers to total personnel) were directly related to technical complexity. With other structural features (the span of control of the first line supervisor, for example) the greatest divergence lay between the extremes of technology (taken together) and mass production in the middle.[9]

The attention which these writers gave to technology has led to a number of other attempts to categorize industrial organizations in similar terms. Perrow, for example, suggests a fourfold typology in terms of two dimensions: whether the raw materials are standardized or varied, and whether the problem solving 'search' procedures in the organization are analysable and routine or not.[10] Hickson and his colleagues distinguish between 'operations technology' (the equipping and sequencing of activities in the workflow), 'materials technology' (the uniformity of materials used) and 'knowledge technology' (the proportion of exceptional cases). Their own studies have led them to emphasize the importance of one aspect of operations technology, 'workflow integration'—the degree to which there is an automated, continuous, fixed sequence of operations.[11]

MODIFICATIONS OF THE TECHNOLOGICAL IMPLICATIONS APPROACH

Whatever the conceptualization of technology, this approach

[8] For example Woodward, *Management and Technology, op. cit.*, p. 29.

[9] Woodward, *op. cit.*

[10] C. Perrow, *Organizational Analysis: a Sociological View* (Tavistock, 1970), especially pp. 75–91.

[11] D. J. Hickson *et al.*, 'Operations Technology and Organizational Structure: An Empirical Reappraisal', *Administrative Science Quarterly*, 14, 1969, pp. 378–97.

to the explanation of social relations in industry implies basically that technology determines, or narrowly constrains, the role structure of the organization which in turn determines or constrains social relations, attitudes and behaviour. This set of assumptions has been questioned in a variety of ways. In their more recent work, for example, Woodward and her colleagues have argued that in differentiating types of batch production firms the most important variable is the degree of uncertainty they have to cope with, and this is dependent on both technology and the control system of the organization.[12] In a large-scale comparative study of a sample of work organizations, including thirty-one manufacturing units, Hickson and his colleagues have found no evidence to support the hypothesis that operations technology is of primary importance to structure; size was much more important. After having tested their own and what they take to be Woodward's formulation of the technology variable they concluded:

'Structural variables will be associated with operations technology only where they are centred on the workflow. The smaller the organization the more its structure will be pervaded by such technological effects; the larger the organization, the more these effects will be confined to variables such as job-counts of employees on activities linked with the workflow itself, and will not be detectable in variables of the more remote administrative and hierarchical structure.'[13]

The link between technology and social structure has however been reformulated in a more fundamental way in terms of the socio-technical systems approach, and radically attacked by proponents of an 'action approach' in industrial sociology.

Socio-technical systems and organizational choice

Probably the most theoretically sophisticated discussion of the importance of technology is to be found in the development by members of the Tavistock Institute of Human Relations of the concept of 'socio-technical systems'[14] as a framework for research:

'The concept of socio-technical system arose from the consideration that any production system requires both a technological

[12] J. Woodward (ed.), *Industrial Organization: Behaviour and Control* (Oxford University Press, 1970).

[13] D. J. Hickson *et al.*, *op. cit.*; see also J. Child, 'More Myths of Management Organization?', *Journal of Management Studies*, 7, 1970, pp. 382-3.

[14] F. E. Emery and E. L. Trist, 'Socio-Technical Systems', in F. E. Emery (ed.), *Systems Thinking* (Penguin, 1969).

organization—equipment and process layout—and a work organ-ization relating to each other those who carry out the necessary tasks. The technological demands place limits on the type of work organization possible, but a work organization has social and psychological properties of its own that are independent of technology . . . A socio-technical system must also satisfy the financial conditions of the industry of which it is a part . . . It has in fact social, technological and economic dimensions, all of which are interdependent but all of which have independent values of their own.'[15]

A socio-technical system is regarded as an 'open' rather than a 'closed' system: it is related to its environment by exchange processes and is able to achieve a 'steady state' from differing initial conditions and in different ways.

The socio-technical systems concept was used initially in studies of coal mining in Britain and the cotton industry in India.[16] The implication of both these studies was that in a given techno-logical situation there is a degree of 'organizational choice', that is, the grouping of tasks into roles and the social relations between role-occupants could be varied quite considerably. The choice made by management was seen as being dependent on certain assumptions as to what would prove most efficient. In both cases the choices had been made in terms of accepted production engineering assumptions: the desirability of a high degree of task specialization, the possibility of treating workers as isolated individuals, and the advisability of keeping planning, co-ordinating and control functions divorced from the work group. The Tavi-stock researchers advocated the deliberate creation of work groups (in the mining case of as many as forty men) consisting of workers able to perform several tasks, and the restoring to these groups of a measure of 'responsible autonomy' so that they could regulate and co-ordinate their own activities, their pay being related to the quantity and quality of output. Changes along these lines were made in both situations and resulted in marked improve-ments in productivity and morale.

This emphasis on the possibility and importance of the choice of social organization within given technological constraints has been made by other writers. Child, for example, also points out

[15] E. L. Trist, et al., Organizational Choice (Tavistock, 1963).
[16] Ibid.; A. K. Rice, Productivity and Social Organization (Tavistock, 1958); A. K. Rice, The Enterprise and its Environment (Tavistock, 1963). For further discussion see R. K. Brown, 'Research and Consultancy in Industrial Enterprises', Sociology, 1, 1967, pp. 30–60.

that the 'strategic choices' made by 'dominant coalitions' in organizations are not only influenced by factors such as technology and size, but also reflect their own preferences and perceptions of the situation and their ability to influence their environment. Any choice may be a compromise between conflicting priorities.[17] Indeed more recent work by members of the Tavistock Institute has highlighted the difficulties in many situations of securing the same sort of correspondence between 'task groups' and 'sentient groups' (the socially supportive 'informal' groups) as was possible in the mining and cotton industry studies.[18] Social organization can no longer be regarded as straightforwardly determined by any one or two factors.

Orientation to work

The second line of criticism of the technological implications approach has been more concerned with the assumed relationship between particular role structures, technologically determined or not, and attitudes and behaviour, and has emphasized the importance of the expectations and 'orientations to work' of the actors themselves in any explanation of social relations in industry. In a relatively early study, for example, the absence of the expected relationship between 'task attributes' and attitudes and behaviour led to the suggestion that although workers with town backgrounds did prefer more complex and intrinsically interesting jobs, workers with 'big city' backgrounds had different 'motivational predispositions' and sought the highest pay possible on the least demanding tasks.[19] The stress on the importance of the actor's definition of the situation, therefore, is a criticism of the Human Relations and technological implications approaches.

The most direct criticism of the technological implications approach from this point of view came in an area where it seemed strongest, the automobile assembly line. A large number of studies had emphasized the way in which this production system inevitably produced highly fragmented and repetitive tasks, with little intrinsic satisfaction, severely restricted the formation of sociable groupings of any kind, accentuated management–worker differences, placed the worker under considerable pressure to

[17] J. Child, op. cit.; J. Child, 'Organizational Structure, Environment and Performance—The Role of Strategic Choice', Sociology, 6, 1972.

[18] E. Miller and A. K. Rice, Systems of Organization (Tavistock, 1967).

[19] A. Turner and P. Lawrence, Industrial Jobs and the Worker, (Cambridge, Mass.: Harvard University Press, 1966).

maximise output and provided few possibilities of promotion or rewards other than relatively high pay.[20] There were certain anomalous findings however: Guest had shown how the succession of a new manager could lead to an improvement in industrial and interpersonal relations;[21] Turner and his colleagues argued that technology could not explain the different strike records of motor car companies in Britain using the same system of production;[22] and others had advocated job enlargement, job rotation, or the appropriate style of supervisory leadership, as leading to increased social satisfaction for workers.[23]

In the course of studying 'affluent workers' in three firms in Luton, Goldthorpe and his colleagues discovered that although assembly line workers did dislike the actual tasks they had to perform this was not associated with any marked dissatisfaction with the job, with the firm as an employer or with management and supervisors. These workers did not look for close social relations with fellow workers nor for supportive supervision; a good supervisor was someone who would leave them alone. The researchers explained these findings as being due to the workers' instrumental orientation to work, seeking a high level of economic rewards at work for expenditure on their homes and families which were the central interest of their lives. This explanation was supported by the finding that in the other two factories studied, a process production chemical plant and a batch production engineering factory, the same orientation to work was associated with similar attitudes and behaviour despite the technological differences.[24]

Goldthorpe and his colleagues suggest that orientations to work are largely formed outside the factory—being influenced in the case of the 'affluent workers' by their family, community and class situations; and that in conditions of full employment workers will tend to choose their place of work in terms of their

[20] C. R. Walker and R. H. Guest, *Man on the Assembly Line* (Cambridge, Mass.: Harvard University Press, 1952); E. Chinoy, *Automobile Workers and the American Dream* (Garden City, New York: Doubleday, 1955).

[21] R. H. Guest, *Organizational Change* (Homewood, Ill.: Dorsey Press, 1962).

[22] H. A. Turner et al., *Labour Relations in the Motor Industry* (Allen and Unwin, 1967).

[23] G. Friedmann, *op. cit.*, especially pp. 40–54; E. Chinoy, 'Manning the Machine—the Assembly Line Worker', in P. L. Berger (ed.), *The Human Shape of Work* (New York: Macmillan, 1964), pp. 51–81; C. R. Walker et al., *The Foreman on the Assembly Line* (Cambridge, Mass.: Harvard University Press, 1956).

[24] J. H. Goldthorpe, 'Attitudes and Behaviour of Car Assembly Workers: A Deviant Case and A Theoretical Critique', *British Journal of Sociology*, 7, 1966, pp. 227–44; J. H. Goldthorpe et al., *The Affluent Worker: Industrial Attitudes and Behaviour* (Cambridge University Press, 1968).

orientations, leading to largely self-selected workforces with shared expectations. Thus, attitudes and behaviour at work must be explained by reference to non-work factors and not in terms of the social system of the factory itself. This line of argument has received support from Ingham's study of the relationship of size of plant and absence and labour turnover.[25]

Thus the emphasis on 'orientations to work', and actors' expectations and definitions of the situation, makes it unlikely that any determinant relationship between technology and social relations can be established. The concept of 'orientation to work', however, is not itself entirely without problems. Daniel has suggested that explanations of choice of job, behaviour in a job and leaving a job are likely to be different. He points to the dangers and difficulties inherent in 'making central to one's enquiries something so elusive and intangible as the actor's subjective definition of work'; and argues, for example, that favourable attitudes towards a foreman because he left workers alone could reflect a desire for autonomy rather than an instrumental orientation.[26]

More important, it cannot be suggested that orientations to work are necessarily, or even normally, as stable and as independent of the work situation as Goldthorpe and colleagues argue. This may well be the case only with instrumentally-oriented workers. Workers with more affective involvement in work are likely to modify their orientation as a result of work experiences. Baldamus, for example, has outlined the process of secondary socialization which leads to common definitions of 'fair pay'.[27] Further, in a study of shipbuilding workers it was argued that not only does the industry, with its craft technology and traditions, dominate the communities from which workers are recruited, and in which they derive many of their expectations of work, but these workers' social perspectives can only be understood in terms of their work *and* community situations.[28] If orientations to work are directly or indirectly influenced by the experience of work, technological differences must continue to be regarded as of potential

[25] G. K. Ingham, 'Organizational Size, Orientation to Work and Industrial Behaviour', *Sociology*, 1, 1967, pp. 239–58; G. K. Ingham, *Size of Industrial Organization and Worker Behaviour* (Cambridge University Press, 1970).
[26] W. W. Daniel, 'Industrial Behaviour and Orientation to Work—a Critique', *Journal of Management Studies*, 6, 1969, pp. 366–75; J. H. Goldthorpe replied in the same journal, 7, 1970, pp. 199–208.
[27] W. Baldamus, *Efficiency and Effort* (Tavistock, 1961).
[28] R. K. Brown and P. Brannen, 'Social Relations and Social Perspectives amongst Shipbuilding Workers—a preliminary statement', *Sociology*, 4, 1970, pp. 71–84, 197–211.

importance in explaining differences in social relations, attitudes and behaviour.

TECHNICAL CHANGE AND RESISTANCE TO CHANGE

Major technical changes are bound to have important repercussions on social relations within industrial organizations, and indeed outside them as well. Where changes involve a transition from one type of production system to another, Woodward suggests, on the basis of a number of case studies, that either changes take place to make social relations compatible with the demands of the new system, or predictable organizational problems arise due to resistance to change.[29] With some exceptions, detailed investigations of technical change have tended to be case studies and it is often difficult to assess their importance and value as a basis for generalization. Some valuable attempts have been made to systematize the work that has been done in this area,[30] but it is only possible to summarize here some of the factors which appear to be important and to give examples from case studies.

As Burns and Stalker have pointed out, industrial organizations can be conceived as comprising not only a 'working organization', but a 'status structure' and a 'political system' as well.[31] Technical changes are likely to affect not only the tasks to be done and work role relationships, but also the absolute and relative rewards and status of different groups and individuals, and their power and autonomy within the organization. In general it can be argued that resistance to change will occur when group or individual interests are threatened, including power and status in the organization. The degree to which this is true, and the particular manifestations of resistance to change will, however, be influenced by a variety of other factors.

The most important of these appears to be the definition of the situation by those affected, for example, the extent to which management's power to make changes is accepted as legitimate and/or likely to be used in employees' interests. Thus in this area of study an 'action approach' is certainly appropriate. Orientations to change tend to be more favourable among workers who are younger, more highly educated and with a higher occupational

---

[29] Woodward, *Industrial Organization, op. cit.*, 1965, especially pp. 209–40.

[30] A. Touraine *et al.*, *Workers' Attitudes to Technical Change* (Paris: OECD, 1965).

[31] T. Burns and G. M. Stalker, *The Management of Innovation* (Tavistock, 1961).

status.[32] The way in which changes are introduced is also important; conditions of secrecy, with no information until a late stage, are likely to give rise to greater anxiety and resistance to change than are cases where information is given, or even more so where those involved participate in planning the changes.[33] A major change in production system may well meet with more resistance than mere improvements of existing processes.

Since the days of the Luddites there has been opposition to changes which threaten the very existence of an occupational group, especially one with craft skills. With more advanced and integrated production systems it has been suggested that worker and union action tends to move to the level of the industry, or the whole economy, to safeguard their interests, rather than trying vainly to prevent changes in a particular plant.[34] It has also been suggested that change is more difficult to introduce in certain types of organization than others, in particular where the firm is either dominated by one group or thoroughly integrated and harmonious.

Studies of technical change in the steel industry illustrate a number of points. In a North Wales steel plant, for example, a series of major innovations proceeded very smoothly with full consultation with the unions. On the whole, however, no occupational group was seriously adversely affected by the changes. Redundancy was avoided because of the wartime shortage of labour and, later, the expansion of the plant. Management prerogatives were clearly defined and accepted as legitimate, as was the seniority principle in promoting workers. Management–union relations were harmonious and workers' interests were effectively represented, in the case of the process workers largely by lay officials.[35]

In contrast a situation where technical changes were being introduced during a recession in the North East steel industry

[32] A. Touraine et al., op. cit., especially pp. 135–48; Department of Social Science, University of Liverpool, Men, Steel and Technical Change, Problems of Progress in Industry No. 1 (HMSO, 1957), pp. 20–7.

[33] Cf. for example E. Mumford and O. Banks, The Computer and the Clerk (Routledge, 1967); L. Coch and J. R. P. French, Jun., 'Overcoming Resistance to Change', Human Relations, 1948, pp. 512–32.

[34] A. Touraine et al., op. cit., pp. 40–2, 87.

[35] Department of Social Science, op. cit.; W. H. Scott et al., Technical Change and Industrial Relations (Liverpool: University Press, 1956); O. Banks, The Attitudes of Steelworkers to Technical Change (Liverpool: University Press, 1960); see also R. K. Brown, 'Participation, Conflict and Change in Industry', Sociological Review, 1965, pp. 273–95.

did give rise to a number of conflicts between management and workers. These could be seen, however, as being concerned with claims for compensation for 'real' losses due to the effects of technical change, and as part of the process of formulating new principles to govern social relations at plant level in the changed situation.[36]

There are similarities too between the North Wales steel plant and the findings of a study of changes in the South Wales tinplate industry from hand rolling to automated production. In both cases management organization became more complex, specialized, and formal, and in many ways more remote; and the relative functional importance of process workers and maintenance craftsmen shifted to the advantage of the latter. In both cases too attitudes towards the changes could only be understood in terms of the *relative* satisfactions and 'deprivations they brought; in the tinplate industry, for example, appreciation of physically lighter work was outweighed by dissatisfaction at the loss of autonomy on the job on the part of the cohesive, largely self-selected, interdependent task groups, which had existed in the hand-rolling plant.[37]

AUTOMATION

Much of the interest in technical change in recent years has been centred on automation. This term has been used to mean many things, and very varied and contradictory assertions have been made about the likely consequences of these latest technological developments. In fact automation is used to refer to at least three 'independent streams of technical progress': the use of transfer devices to link machine tools in automatic production lines; the development of techniques of automatic control over manufacturing process; and the use of computers for data processing, with the possibility of the extension of automatic control over complex operations. The last two streams, which involve the 'mechanization of sensory control and thought processes', are what is often meant by full automation.[38] The consequences for social relations within industrial organizations will depend on both the pre-existing situation and the type of automation introduced.

In general it has been argued that automation describes the same sort of technology and associated social relations as have

[36] J. E. T. Eldridge, 'Plant Bargaining in Steel', *Sociological Review*, 13, 1965, pp. 131–48; and *Industrial Disputes* (Routledge, 1968).
[37] J. Chadwick-Jones, *Automation and Behaviour* (Wiley-Interscience, 1969).
[38] P. Sadler, *Social Research on Automation* (Heinemann, 1968).

been described above as process production. Thus mechanization and rationalization of processes are fully developed and operations centre on monitoring and maintaining the plant rather than direct production work. Work groups are small, responsible and relatively autonomous. Management–worker relations tend to be harmonious; the plant itself provides discipline and control and labour costs are a smaller proportion of total costs (though still one which management can influence). Supervisory ratios tend to increase, management organizations may become more complex and there is concern with the coordination of different aspects of production operations. At the same time, rational decision making on the basis of knowledge and technical expertise becomes increasingly possible.[39] The reservations about the social implications of technology in general apply to automation also; Smith, for example, has pointed out that whether autonomy of work roles is experienced as such by the operative is dependent upon several factors including the worker's sense of identity.[40]

In contrast to the general picture, the use of semi-automatic production systems, such as transfer machines in the car industry (hence 'Detroit automation'), has been shown by Faunce to result in the dispersal of work groups, greater pace of work, less frequent interaction with fellow workers, more pressure from supervisors and considerable strain involved in monitoring expensive equipment in a highly integrated process, even though the work was physically lighter.[41] In another case the introduction of a semi-automatic tube mill similarly meant that fewer workers were more widely dispersed, though the public address system was used for gossip as well as its intended purpose. Work roles were, however, highly interdependent because of the integrated process and strong group feeling developed. Initially the demands of operating the new plant caused considerable strain and anxiety, but this disappeared as the men mastered their new work environment. Also, there was conflict at first regarding the incentive scheme and, though this was resolved, relationships with maintenance staff, who were not included but whose contribution was vital, remained troublesome.[42]

[39] See for example Blauner, *op. cit.*; F. C. Mann and L. R. Hoffman, *Automation and the Worker* (New York: Holt Dryden, 1960); F. E. Emery and J. Marek, 'Some Socio-technical Aspects of Automation', *Human Relations*, 1962, pp. 17–25.

[40] M. A. Smith, 'Process Technology and Powerlessness', *British Journal of Sociology*, 1968, pp. 76–88.

[41] W. A. Faunce, 'Automation in the Automobile Industry', in S. Marcson (ed.), *Automation, Alienation and Anomie* (New York: Harper, 1970).

[42] C. R. Walker, *Towards the Automatic Factory* (New Haven: Yale University Press, 1957); see also J. Chadwick-Jones, *op. cit.*

The situation is different when office automation—electronic data processing—is considered, though as yet there is only a limited amount of research available.[43] Some routine jobs disappear, but routine operations connected with the computer, for example preparing information for it, increase in number, and workers engaged on these, generally women, tend to be fairly sharply divided from those, generally men, in more responsible positions and with prospects of promotion. Especially where computers are used to perform qualitatively new tasks (rather than just conventional tasks previously done by a large number of clerks, such as calculating wages), their introduction may cause major modifications to the distribution of power in the firm, and their full use may be resisted for this reason. Areas of uncertainty are reduced, more centralized decision making becomes possible, and there is greater dependence on the experts associated with the computer installation; the middle levels of management in particular may well lose control over a number of areas previously under their discretion.

This second, 'integrated', stage of office automation, combined with the technological advances associated with the other two streams of automation, may, it is suggested, lead to a type of industrial organization where authority is objectively and rationally used and decisions are not even in part the result of political bargaining within the enterprise. Though trends towards such a situation are observable, Willener has argued that at least two issues will remain: 'the suspicion that the system favours certain occupational or social categories'; and 'the problem of policy—the orientation given to the common activities'.[44]

Automation can be regarded as the latest of a long line of technical changes; study of it can add to our knowledge of the processes of change in industrial organizations. This is not to deny, however, that the development of these various trends may lead to qualitatively new types of situation within industrial organizations.

[43] H. A. Rhee, *Office Automation in Social Perspective* (Oxford: Blackwell, 1968); E. Mumford and O. Banks, *op. cit.*
[44] A. Touraine *et al., op. cit.*, pp. 86–7.

CHAPTER 10

Management

IT has become accepted in recent years that management can make an important contribution to economic prosperity, and there has consequently been a growing interest in management education. Two perspectives of management have been highlighted. The first is a view of management as an economic resource performing a set of technical administrative functions. The second is of an élite social group to which the process of management education offers a basis for special competence as well as a system of selective entry. Less attention, however, has been given to a third perspective, that of management as a system of power and authority within which different personal and group strategies are pursued. This political aspect of management necessarily qualifies both a formal view of managerial functions and the assumption that managers comprise and identify with a distinctive élite or class within the social structure. The present chapter seeks to develop this qualification by examining studies of managers' orientations and actions.[1]

Management in the social structure

The question of how managers are located within the occupational and stratification systems of modern industrial societies has provided a major point of sociological debate.[2] This issue has been brought into prominence by evidence suggesting that 'management' has grown during this century into an occupation of some significance throughout industrialized societies. As we

[1] These three perspectives on management are elaborated by F. H. Harbison and C. A. Myers, *Management in the Industrial World* (New York: McGraw-Hill, 1959). They are reflected in the distinction between 'working organization', 'status structure' and 'political system' drawn by T. Burns and G. M. Stalker, *The Management of Innovation* (Tavistock, 1961).
[2] See T. Nichols, *Ownership, Control and Ideology* (Allen & Unwin, 1969), especially Chapter XII.

indicated in Chapter 2, the increasing proportion of managerial along with white-collar and technical staff to manual employees appears to have represented a general trend in industry and it is estimated that in the United Kingdom, for instance, about 1·8 million people occupied managerial jobs in 1971, accounting for 6·2% of total employment.[3]

Not only have the numbers of people in managerial positions grown, but other developments appear to indicate that management has become increasingly differentiated both from business owners and from other employees. Differentiation from ownership has been expressed by the concept of a 'divorce of ownership from control', in which the effective control of business organizations is seen to have passed from the hands of an increasingly fragmented and absentee body of shareholders to full-time executives. Quite naturally this proposition has stimulated considerable speculation as to the social identity, motivations and goals of the new managerial controllers.[4] The factors which are held to have encouraged this trend—increasing scale, capital intensification and technical complexity—have in general established requirements for a higher level of technical and administrative sophistication among managers. This is also cited as the main reason for the differentiation of management from other levels of employment through the application of increasingly selective entrance requirements. Thus the proportion of senior level managers with a university education has risen considerably faster in both Britain and the United States over the past few decades than has the proportion of graduates in their populations as a whole.[5] Studies of British managers indicate that men with higher educational qualifications and social origins are today heavily represented in managerial positions.[6]

A distinct and relatively homogeneous occupational identity among managers would seem to be manifested in the development of a specialized institutional framework and to be underpinned by an extensive body of ideology. The establishment of management institutes has reflected a view that managers required their own quasi-professional associations apart from already existing

[3] Census 1971 England & Wales (HMSO).
[4] For a discussion and review of evidence on the 'divorce of ownership from control', see J. Child, The Business Enterprise in Modern Industrial Society (Collier-Macmillan, 1969), Chapter III.
[5] Acton Society Trust, Management Succession, 1956, p. 15; W. L. Warner and J. C. Abegglen, Big Business Leaders in America (New York: Harper, 1955), p. 47.
[6] D. G. Clark, The Industrial Manager—His Background and Career Pattern (Business Publications, 1966), Chapters 3 and 4. Also P. Stanworth and A. Giddens (eds.), Elites and Power in British Society (Cambridge University Press, 1974).

employers' organizations. The ideology which developed, partly through the activities of management institutes, laid heavy emphasis on the argument that managers had emerged as a separate occupational group in their own right and theories were elaborated which provided management with its own basis of legitimation. The dominant theme in this ideology thus presented managers as embodying a happy marriage of professional expertise with a social conscience unfettered by prior loyalties to sectional owning interests.[7]

It is not altogether surprising that this combination of developments—functional differentiation, selectivity of entry, institutional organization and ideology—should have been widely regarded as signalling the emergence of a new class in modern industrial societies. Indeed, the discussion of management techniques and the exchange of ideological assumptions between spokesmen in different countries suggested that managers were assuming a common social identity, even at an international level. The apparent trend towards a concentration of business control into the hands of a new self-selective managerial élite within larger enterprises, together with the other developments mentioned, lent face validity to influential theses of the 'managerial revolution' expounded since the 1930s. More recently, Galbraith has claimed that the expansion of managerial and technical expertise has led to control in organizations effectively passing down from top managers to groups of experts comprising the 'technostructure'. In Galbraith's view we are in this way passing beyond even the managerial revolution.[8]

The foregoing line of argument, which Nichols has aptly labelled 'managerialism', relies however upon certain questionable assumptions.[9] Most importantly, it tends to utilize evidence of a division of functions between managers and owners in support of the proposition that the interests, identities and social reference groups of the two parties have diverged to an important degree. There are good reasons to doubt the extent to which this has been the case, particularly among the higher levels of management

[7] For British developments see J. Child, British Management Thought (Allen & Unwin, 1969). An excellent analysis of the early development of management is A. Tillett, 'Industry and Management', in Tillett et al. (eds.), Management Thinkers (Penguin, 1970), Part I.

[8] Cf. A. A. Berle and G. C. Means, The Modern Corporation and Private Property (New York: Macmillan, 1933); J. Burnham, The Managerial Revolution (New York: Day, 1941 (also Penguin)); J. K. Galbraith, The New Industrial State (Penguin, 1969).

[9] Nichols, op. cit., Part I.

where, *pace* Galbraith, the locus of policy-making generally still remains. [There is evidence that senior managers have by and large remained integrated with wider business interests both normatively and in terms of social relationships.] In addition to this common identification, the ability of management to pursue policies at variance with ownership interests remains constrained by the continued reliance of many companies upon external financing and by the now growing concentration of large company share-ownership into the hands of financial institutions. So, with respect at least to identity and action, there are a number of considerations which together cast doubt upon the notion that top management today constitutes a class differentiated from the broader, albeit somewhat amorphous, business class as a whole.[10]

Managerialist theories also contain the implicit assumption that managers constitute a relatively homogeneous social group. The term 'management' is indeed frequently employed to denote a group of people who share common interests and a common social identity. This assumption is also open to challenge. So much so that one is led to question the utility of employing a concept such as 'manager' in any other than the technical sense of administrative science. For research into managerial orientations and actions demonstrates how significantly managers diverge among themselves. Not only is this research in general relevant to the organizational and role level of analysis with which this part of the book is concerned, but it raises in particular the problem of in what sense management can be distinguished as a single group within the social structure.

Variety in managerial orientations

From a sociological point of view, it is of little significance to classify managers together simply by virtue of the nature of their tasks which themselves may be common only at a relatively trivial level of generality.[11] Rather, it is a manager's location within cultural value systems, his education and professional training, and his position within the network of activities and relationships in an organization which are sociologically of greater significance, for these factors point to some of the major influences upon his

[10] Child, *The Business Enterprise, op. cit.*, Chapter III, where other assumptions underpinning the managerialist argument are critically examined including the degree to which practising managers have accepted 'managerial ideology'.

[11] I.e., the triviality of the truism that management is 'working through people', or of Fayol's 'classic' definition: 'to manage is to forecast and plan, to organize, to command, to co-ordinate and to control', H. Fayol, *General and Industrial Management* (Pitman, 1949), pp. 5-6.

orientation (his general set of attitudes and expectations) towards the organization and his behaviour within it. Differences in managers' social and cultural locations appear to make for quite considerable differences in personal orientation and behaviour. Interest has grown recently in the study of cross-cultural differences between managers, or 'comparative management'.[12] Particularly striking differences have been found between managers in highly industrialized societies such as the United Kingdom and the USA and those in developing countries. For example Lauterbach studied managerial attitudes in five South American countries and he concluded that 'work habits of management . . . are quite different from those in North America or Western Europe . . . what is really involved is a different way of looking at life in general and at economic activities in particular'. McClelland measured the motivation of managers in the United States and in three other progressively less industrialized regions—North Italy, South Italy and Turkey—together with Poland. The sample of American managers expressed the greatest need for achievement and for exercising power, and the least need (Poland apart) for good relations with other people. McClelland suggests that these results, together with differences in attitudes which he found between his samples of managers, are associated with the stage of economic development in the society from which the managers are drawn. Insofar as this is a causal factor it is likely to make itself felt through the different social value systems of the societies concerned. Haire, Ghiselli and Porter, in another comparative study, also found that there were differences between managers regarding the extent and the manner in which they felt their personal needs were satisfied. They concluded that the explanation lay in socio-cultural factors, especially the place that the manager held in his country's occupational status hierarchy and the influence that business had on the political affairs of each country.[13]

Although Haire, Ghiselli and Porter concluded that managerial orientations in Britain and in the United States could be said to form a single group in contrast to those in other countries, substantial differences in such orientations have been identified,

[12]Two useful reviews are R. A. Webber, *Culture and Management: Text and Readings in Comparative Management* (Homewood, Ill.: Irwin, 1969); R. Nath, 'A Methodological review of Cross-Cultural Management Research', *International Social Science Journal*, XX, January 1968, pp. 35–61.

[13] A. Lauterbach, 'Managerial Attitudes in Western South America', in *Managerial Attitudes in Chile* (Santiago: University of Chile, 1961), p. 183; D. C. McClelland, *The Achieving Society* (New York: Van Nostrand, 1961), pp. 287–92; M. Haire *et al.*, *Managerial Thinking* (New York: Wiley, 1966).

at least impressionistically, even between these two highly industrialized and to a degree culturally similar societies. Dubin has recently concluded that in contrast to American managers, those in Britain place less value on change and innovation, less value on professionalism, are inclined to allocate resources within an organization according to people's status rather than their needs, are inclined to place high values upon personal trust and to employ personalistic rather than universalistic criteria in evaluating others. Recruitment to British management, Dubin argues, relies on a system of education that makes rather improbable the direct entrance of lower middle-class and working-class men into executive ranks. Once there, promotion is largely on the basis of age rather than of talent, while the personal pursuit of advancement through mobility between companies is frowned upon. In other words, in Britain upward managerial mobility tends to be *ascribed* while in the United States it tends to be *achieved*. Dubin is not alone in making this kind of comparison between American and British or European managers. He regards the orientations and behaviour of British managers as a manifestation of a British industrial culture which itself reflects wider social norms, but which poses 'a major barrier to the rapid and full flowering of industrial creativity'.[14]

Another aspect of differences in orientations between British and American managers is brought to light by the available studies on how they use their leisure-time. For many American managers, leisure-time seems to represent an 'extension' of work in that it is infused by considerations relating to a job which represents a dominant interest in their lives. In contrast, for many British managers, leisure appears to assume more of a 'neutral' relationship to work. Most of British managers' relatively more generous time off from work appears to be spent in 'privatized' activities. These differences may well reflect not only contrasting values given to work and achievement by the managerially-relevant reference groups in the two societies, but also the reduced opportunities for self-fulfilment in British manager's jobs implied by Dubin's observations.[15]

[14] R. Dubin, 'Management in Britain—Impressions of a Visiting Professor', *Journal of Management Studies*, 7, 1970, pp. 183-98; also F. H. Harbison and C. A. Myers, *op. cit.*; O. H. Nowotny, 'American *vs.* European Management Philosophy', *Harvard Business Review*, March–April 1964, pp. 101-8. Turner has distinguished similar differences in norms between the American and British educational processes, R. H. Turner, 'Modes of Social Ascent through Education: Sponsored and Contest Mobility', *American Sociological Review*, XXV, 1960, pp. 855-67.

[15] J. Child and B. Macmillan, 'Managerial Leisure in British and American Contexts', *Journal of Management Studies*, May 1972.

Managerial orientations may reflect in the ways illustrated the values of the communities in which managers are located, but they are also likely to reflect their place within that community in the sense of their specialist occupational training and membership. Differences in the attitudes and ideologies held by members of different occupations have been frequently noted by sociologists.[16] These are relevant to an understanding of managers in that the 'management' of a particular organization is itself likely to comprise an amalgam of specialized, sometimes professional, occupational groups. This occupational differentiation within management is growing along with the rising sophistication of relevant techniques, the growing complexity of products and services, and the average size of work organizations. Moore noted this development some while ago and he concluded that it tended to introduce sources of tension and strain between the various management groups.[17]

Orientations can vary significantly between the different specialized members of management groups. Results from the writer's own research serve to reinforce this point because they concern the attitudes of managers at a senior (departmental head and director) level where one would have expected the greatest degree of consensus in orientations to have developed. Among a sample of 787 such managers in six British industries, personal orientations to matters such as variety in work environment, taking risks and retaining an open mind about the solution to problems, were all significantly different as between managers in charge of ten major functional areas.[18] Research, personnel and marketing managers tended to exhibit the greatest flexibility of mind in regard to these matters, while financial managers and quality control managers exhibited the least mental flexibility. When it came to expectations of how they and their fellow managers should in general behave, the differences between managers in different functions were also all highly significant statistically, particularly in regard to items concerning the challenging of formal authority and procedure. A similar pattern of results again emerged in that financial and quality control managers were in this respect the most 'conservative' groups, while

[16] Cf. S. Nosow and W. H. Form (eds.), *Man, Work and Society* (New York: Basic Books, 1962), Chapter XII.

[17] W. E. Moore, 'Occupational Structure and Industrial Conflict', in W. Kornhauser, R. Dubin and A. Ross (eds.), *Industrial Conflict* (New York: McGraw-Hill, 1954).

[18] T. Ellis and J. Child, 'Placing Stereotypes of the Manager into Perspective', *Journal of Management Studies*, 10, October 1973.

marketing, personnel, research and also production managers formed the most 'radical' groups.

These fairly systematic differences in attitudes between functional groups within management may reflect not only the influence of prior occupational socialization and a continued contact with external occupational reference groups, but also the different roles performed by such groups within the system of operations in their organizations. For the managers who exhibited more rigid and conservative attitudes are placed in a predominantly monitoring and 'controlling' role, while the contrasting groups generally comprised managers who had an important 'initiating' function within the organization.

The continued attachment of specialists in management to wider occupational reference groups may in fact be facilitated by their location within the operating system of an organization. Insofar as the formal role of specialist managers is to take charge of work to which specialized techniques, professional conventions, or scientific modes of analysis are applied, they are obliged to retain close contact with outside institutions and groups as sources of useful knowledge and points of comparative reference. One would expect the location in this sense of managers on the 'boundary' of an organization to reinforce any tendency towards what Gouldner has called a 'cosmopolitan' orientation. This orientation is one of commitment to professional contact outside any particular organization in which the manager is employed, and it contrasts with the 'local' orientation towards the one organization which may be found more frequently among managers concerned with the 'technological core' of its activities.[19]

As well as his position in respect of the organization's boundary, there are indications that a manager's position in the administrative hierarchy and his distance from the main centre of strategic decision-making may influence his orientations towards the official policies laid down for the organization. Thus foremen, who in this respect may be said to occupy the lowest level of management, have been found to represent their subordinates' point of view against that of senior management, particularly where union organization was weak.[20] Porter and Lawler concluded from a review of their own and other studies that the job satisfaction of

---

[19] A. W. Gouldner, 'Cosmopolitans and Locals', *Administrative Science Quarterly*, December 1957–March 1958, pp. 281–306, 444–80. On the concept of 'technological core', see J. D. Thompson, *Organizations in Action* (New York: McGraw-Hill, 1967).

 [20] K. E. Thurley and A. C. Hamblin, *The Supervisor and his Job* (HMSO, 1963), pp. 15–16.

managers was positively related to occupying a high position in the hierarchy. The substance of this relationship is itself likely to encourage, and may also reflect, different orientations towards work and the organization.[21].

The particular 'character' of the organization in which a manager works may constitute an influence upon his general outlook which is thereby differentiated in a further respect from that of other managers. As Sofer has commented in reviewing relevant research, 'stereotypes often develop about what members of a particular organization are like, influencing expectations of such people and their actual behaviour; organizational colleagues support common ideologies and symbols, . . . organizational colleagues will share preoccupations about the success and reputation of the organization and about its internal politics since these involve their shared fate'.[22] Selection processes, induction and training programmes, group pressures, formal procedures and other features may all induce some degree of conformity to an ideology which contrasts with that of other managements.

In short, managerial orientations are diverse. At one level, there is variation between populations of managers in different societies. Within societies, there is variation between different occupational groups in management, and between managers employed in different organizations. A manager's location within an organization, especially his place in the hierarchy, may also be associated with such variation. These contrasting managerial orientations when expressed within an organizational framework of interdependent yet competing relationships, provide an important basis for appreciating modes of managerial behaviour.

Managerial behaviour

The social processes which take place within management remain under-researched compared with those between employees lower in the organizational hierarchy. Much of the available evidence on managerial behaviour is of the rather formalistic type captured by diary studies.[23] In the absence of better evidence, stereotypes still hold sway. Dubin has commented that 'in the

[21] L. W. Porter and E. E. Lawler, 'Properties of Organization Structure in Relation to Job Attitudes and Job Behaviour', *Psychological Bulletin*, 66, 1965, pp. 23-51.

[22] C. Sofer, *Men in Mid-Career: A Study of British Managers and Technical Specialists* (Cambridge University Press, 1970), p. 141.

[23] Reviews of such studies are given in R. Stewart, *Managers and Their Jobs* (Macmillan, 1967), and H. Mintzberg, *The Nature of Managerial Work* (New York: Harper & Row, 1973).

folklore of managerial literature much is made of the need for total immersion of the individual in his organization', and the stereotype of managerial conformity to the norms and expectations established by top policy-makers portrayed in Whyte's 'Organization Man' and similar works probably still remains the most influential portrayal of typical managerial behaviour.[24] A sociologist, however, would expect behaviour in a role to be a function of both the person's general orientation and the way his role is structured by others with whom he interacts. For this reason diversity in managerial orientations, together with the opportunity for pursuing sectional goals offered by the very complexity of modern large-scale organization structures, would lead us to expect a substantial amount of non-conformity with the objectives established by top management and of non-involvement with operations that are not central to the manager's own immediate activities and interests.

Burns and Stalker have pointed out that the pursuit of personal interests and status, with its attendant 'politicking' and struggles for power, form as central a part of behaviour in organizations as does the planning and execution of work itself.[25] Commonly heard catch phrases about the 'management team' obscure this important point. Observers of business decision-making have generally remarked on the significance of the political element, whereby the interests of individuals and organizational groups, together with their likely reactions to alternative outcomes, are assessed and incorporated into the substance of the final decision. The political process not only accounts for the considerable length of time which managements seem to take in reaching major decisions, but also to an extent for the finding that the great majority of their time is spent in talking![26] Studies of conflict within management serve to place this political process in sharp focus, while their analysis of the sources of such conflict provides useful insight into the basis for managerial action in general.

From a participant study of managerial behaviour in four American companies, Dalton concluded that the most dominant social and political forces within an organization are represented

[24] R. Dubin, 'Business Behavior Behaviorally Viewed', in G. B. Strother (ed.), *Social Science Approaches to Business Behavior* (Tavistock, 1962), p. 27; W. H. Whyte, *The Organization Man* (Penguin, 1960); also cf. A. Harrington, *Life in the Crystal Palace* (Cape, 1960).

[25] Burns and Stalker, *op. cit.*

[26] Dubin, *op. cit.*, pp. 24–5; L. R. Sayles, *Managerial Behavior* (New York: McGraw-Hill, 1964), Chapter 12.

by cliques, both aggressive and defensive. Any of these cliques might operate in favour of purely sectional interests within the management as a whole. The political action in which they were involved consisted not only of measures taken in order to protect or expand the clique's sphere of interest, but also counter-measures taken by top management with the intention of maintaining control throughout the management hierarchy. Dalton concluded from his observations that purely formal organization structures and statements of policy are extremely unreliable guides for determining the actual lines of authority and influence.[27]

An important dimension of the political process within management lies along the vertical span of the hierarchy and as such is often bound up with the question of career. The appointment of managers to particular posts, and their career patterns as a whole, usually represent a balancing of technical aspects of personal competence against considerations of internal politics and morale. Thus prospective appointees are likely to have sponsors in senior positions for whom the progress of their protégés is indicative of their own status and influence. In this way, as Sofer points out, careers in large organizations reflect in some degree struggles for power. Apart from power alignments, there are signs that other informal factors may operate in managerial career achievement, including social background, membership of high status clubs, political membership and other elements in normative and relational class conformity. These signposts and gateways on the career path do permit the individual in some degree to 'manage' his own career. However, it would be erroneous to imply that a majority of managers succeed in advancing far up the career ladder and in this fact itself lies an important source of conflict.[28]

For instance, in a factory which stressed promotion as the mark of success, Burns found that older managers lacking further promotion prospects formed themselves into cliques which acted as a protective counter-system against the prevailing norms and values of the organization. Younger managers, in contrast, identified with these norms which were to their advantage and formed their own exclusive 'cabals' in order to promote further occupational success for themselves. The cliques and cabals were in conflict over organizational rewards and status.[29] In another

[27] M. Dalton, *Men who Manage* (New York: Wiley, 1959), Chapter 3.
[28] Sofer, *op. cit.*, pp. 17–22, 56–62.
[29] T. Burns, 'The Reference of Conduct in Small Groups: Cliques and Cabals in Occupational Milieux', *Human Relations*, VIII, November 1955, pp. 467–86.

study, Sykes and Bates described the failure of departmental sales managers to understand and maintain official policy in a large British company. They ascribed this failure primarily to differences in social class background, as well as in status within the company, between more senior general managers and their departmental managerial subordinates, factors which led to a failure of communication between the two groups. The rank of departmental sales manager was the normal limit for a man who had joined the company as a clerk, while the general managers were mainly men with a Public School or University education, who had entered the company as trainee managers. This study thus illustrates how an increasingly selective entry into senior management can not only promote antagonism between levels in the hierarchy, but also render that hierarchy reflective of the system of social stratification prevailing in the wider community.[30] Clements, in his study of British managers, also found that antagonism towards higher management could unsettle more junior managers so much that they considered taking jobs elsewhere.[31]

The various functional groups within management may, as we have seen, hold different orientations derived largely from their respective occupational reference groups. Their orientations and modes of conduct may be further differentiated by virtue of their particular alignments to the operating system of an organization and because of the different environmental conditions to which their activities are linked. This differentiation itself encourages conflict—for instance between production and marketing managers over delivery dates promised to, and the type of orders accepted from, customers. Another well-known case concerns the difficulties in co-operation between research managers and their line counterparts, which Burns and Stalker have analysed in particular detail.[32] They single out a number of factors underlying this type of situation, including the generally contrasting orientations and modes of behaviour of the two groups, inappropriate organizational arrangements leading to 'adaptive segregation' rather than integration between them, and the threat to existing arrangements posed by industrial scientists as agents of change. Hage and Aiken, in their discussion and research on innovation

[30] A. J. M. Sykes and J. Bates, 'A Study of Conflict between Formal Company Policies and the Interests of Informal Groups', *Sociological Review*, 10, November 1962, pp. 313–27

[31] R. V. Clements, *Managers—A Study of Their Careers in Industry* (Allen & Unwin, 1958).

[32] *Op. cit.*

in organizations, conclude that a greater number and diversity of professionals in an organization will help to generate a greater rate of change. On the other hand, the greater the rate of change that is achieved, the more bargaining and conflict between specialist groups over the evaluation and implementation of new proposals there is likely to be.[33]

Dalton has also studied line/staff conflict in American factories, and he has concluded that it is largely attributable to a combination of factors. Some reflected the nature of organizational structure, such as differences in basic functions and the fact that line management approval was necessary for promotion to higher staff positions; some reflected differences in personal frames of reference due to differences in age, formal education, potential occupational ceilings and reference group affiliation; while other factors reflected an underlying process of change such as the fear by line managers that expanding staff groups would undermine their authority.[34] Conflict between managers, then, may derive from various sources: it may reflect fundamental incompatibilities in norms and orientations; it may be a consequence of personal managerial strategies in pursuit of career and status advantage, or it may be the product of little more than an organization structure which encourages poor communication and establishes requirements which are not appropriate to the tasks in hand. Frequently elements of all these factors are operating at the same time.[35]

Dalton's view is that the social process of management within organizations amounts to 'a shifting set of contained and ongoing counter phases of action'.[36] Conflict, of course, represents only one form of such action. Another mode of action which is probably even more prevalent, but less researched, is the reciprocal exchange of favours which Strauss has illustrated in his study of purchasing agents and their adaptation to pressures bearing on their role.[37] Exchange, bargaining and conflict are all manifestations of management as a system of power. The direction, intensity and

[33] J. Hage and M. Aiken, *Social Change in Complex Organizations* (New York: Random House, 1970); also M. Aiken and J. Hage, 'The Organic Organization and Innovation', *Sociology*, 5, January 1971, pp. 63–82.

[34] M. Dalton, 'Conflicts between Line and Staff Managerial Officers', *American Sociological Review*, 15, June 1950, pp. 342–51.

[35] Cf. L. R. Pondy, 'Varieties of Organizational Conflict', *Administrative Science Quarterly*, 14, December 1969, pp. 499–506.

[36] Dalton, *Men Who Manage, op. cit.*, p. 4.

[37] G. Strauss, 'Tactics of Lateral Relationship: The Purchasing Agent', *Administrative Science Quarterly*, 7, September 1962, pp. 161–86.

outcome of power relationships between managers represent a perspective of study which is distinctively sociological and yet has attracted insufficient attention among sociologists. Crozier's study of French bureaucracy is an important exception, and this pointed to uncertainty as having a critical role in the retention of autonomy by departments which alone were able to cope witȟ periodic and unexpected crises.[38] The findings of Hickson and Hinings also suggest that the power of departmental managers 'ensues from coping with uncertainty, provided that what is done has some immediacy to the rest of an organization, and that alternative ways of doing it are not readily available'.[39] The political system bears upon managerial behaviour at all levels and, as Brooke and Remmers have described, it has attained a particularly complex form within multinational enterprises where the continued integration of management assumes the dimensions of a major problem.[40]

Conclusion

We have in this chapter stressed the political aspect of management in focusing upon managers' orientations and strategies. In so doing we have had cause to question the stereotype of management which is found in many writings and in much public discussion—that of formally defined functions executed by socially cohesive teams of men who are conscious of belonging to an identifiable professional élite. A certain measure of reality is probably captured by this stereotype. A degree of common élitist identity may come to be experienced particularly by managers who have received a formal business education. Insofar as 'a reciprocally tolerable meshing of needs and interests between individual and organization' is commonly found,[41] the formal definition of managerial goals and activities is also likely to bear some resemblance to actual behaviour. Nevertheless, the important point is that the political nature of managerial action renders these alternative perspectives of themselves inadequate and problematic.

From the liberal democratic point of view, this is a reassuring conclusion. For it severely qualifies the notion of a rational

[38] M. Crozier, *The Bureaucratic Phenomenon* (Tavistock, 1964).

[39] D. J. Hickson and C. R. Hinings, 'A First Interpretation of Canadian Data on a Strategic Contingencies' Theory of Intra-Organizational Power', paper given to *BSA Industrial Sociology Group*, London, April 1971.

[40] M. Z. Brooke and H. L. Remmers, *The Strategy of Multinational Enterprise* (Longmans, 1970), Chapter 3.

[41] C. Sofer, *op. cit.*, p. 349.

managerial technocracy the actions of which can be held to compare favourably with supposedly 'irrational' or 'irresponsible'
elements in worker behaviour. Secondly, evidence of political
action within management suggests that pressures towards
individual conformity may not in practice have always met with
the success implied by 'organization man'.

CHAPTER 11

Industrial Interest Groups

IT is intended in this chapter to deal with part of the area of study called 'industrial relations', to complete a review of the sociology of industry on the organization-role level. Industrial relations, however, is an extensive field to which many others than sociologists have made contributions from different perspectives— economists, lawyers, psychologists, political scientists, and so on. There is considerable common ground between what these people study and what the sociologist studies, but the approaches are different. The student of industrial relations has a more limited field than the sociologist, but he can regard himself as inter-disciplinary within that field (i.e. he is part economist, part sociologist, part political scientist, and so on). The industrial sociologist has a wider field—which includes industrial relations —but he is not inter-disciplinary and concentrates on using the concepts and theory of sociology. He is particularly interested in *social relations within the enterprise* and the individual, group or collective *expressions of industrial interests*.

TRADE UNIONS AND PROFESSIONAL ASSOCIATIONS

Types of interest group

In the context of industrial relations, interest groups are a special kind of secondary group existing in, or associated with, work organizations with authority structures. In addition to a structure and a form of organization, these groups have a programme or set of goals and a membership which includes among its activities the attempt to further its interests when these conflict with those of other groups. On the side of employees there are trade unions and professional associations, and on the side of employers there are those employers' associations which have industrial relations functions. Although the latter are sometimes regarded as 'the bosses' unions', the parallel is only partial, since the 'employer' is usually an organization that is strong enough to deal directly with the unions, locally if not nationally. Associations of employees, mostly non-manual and sometimes called staff associations, which neither bargain with employers nor represent professional interests are not included here among interest groups.

There are good reasons for analysing the structure, functions and problems facing trade unions and professional associations separately, although they also have some common features. Trade unions are composed mainly of manual workers[1] and their chief function is to bargain with employers over pay and conditions on behalf of their members, a function which is only one of those performed by professional associations on behalf of *their* members. The main problems facing trade unions are the struggle for recognition by employers, the attempts to exert political influence on economic policies at national level in so far as these affect the interests of members,[2] and various internal problems of organization and the need for more funds to extend activities.

Professional associations are composed of those whose employment has gained the recognized status of a profession, whether of the old-established type such as the law, medicine and the church, or of the newer type, including those highly-trained and qualified personnel without the traditional professional-client relationship (sometimes called 'quasi-professionals'). The functions of professional associations are varied: they bestow qualifications as an indication of competence or a licence to practise, they act as study associations, they regulate the professional conduct of their members, and they attempt to protect the interests and raise the status of their members. The main problems facing professional associations are preserving the relationship between the profession and the community, social control of members, adjusting to changes in the traditional professional-client

---

[1] However, there were in 1964 2·6 million members of white-collar unions, an increase of 34% since 1948, during which period union membership as a whole had increased by only 8% to about 10 million. Also, there is a greater potential for white-collar unionism: only 3 out of 10 white-collar workers belong to a union compared with 5 out of 10 manual workers, G. S. Bain, *The Growth of White-Collar Unionism* (Oxford: Clarendon Press, 1970), pp. 21, 37. For a study of unionism in banking see R. M. Blackburn, *Union Character and Social Class* (Batsford, 1967).

[2] The influence of the trade union movement as a whole on government economic policies is exercised by the General Council of the Trades Union Congress, by trade union delegations to the Labour Party Annual Conference, and by individual trade unionist M.P.s.

relationship, and resolving (or at least containing) conflict between sections within the association.

In the light of these differences it has been said that the functions of professional associations and trade unions are mostly kept distinct, with neither showing signs of encroaching on the other.[3] This is true to the extent that many functions of professional associations are not shared by trade unions, but it need not be the case that an individual is *either* a member of a trade union *or* of a professional association. Professional employees are increasingly finding the need to belong to bodies, such as the Association of Scientific, Technical and Managerial Staffs and the Institution of Professional Civil Servants, which will negotiate with their employers over pay and conditions, in addition to whatever professional association they may belong to.

Trade union structure and participation

Considerably more attention has been paid to the organization and membership of trade unions than to that of professional associations. A number of studies have sought to make a sociological analysis of various aspects of trade unionism. Some of the main problems that have received attention are the classification of types of union, the factors influencing member participation, and the associated question of the maintenance of democracy in the functioning of unions.

The traditional classification of trade unions is based on a combination of type of skill and basis of organization into three groups of craft, industrial and general unions. *Craft* unions are the oldest type and are composed of workers performing the same or very similar industrial operations. *Industrial* unions cater for all, skilled and unskilled, within an industry, although the skilled workers tend to dominate this kind of union because they are more organized. *General* unions have members in many industries and are often the result of amalgamations and federations of smaller unions. These types are not always clear-cut; thus the Amalgamated Engineering and Foundry Workers' Union is an industrial union for engineering, but a craft union for engineers and foundry workers in whatever industry they are employed. Also, this classification does not include the non-manual and technicians' unions.

Recognizing that the traditional threefold classification does

[3] K. Prandy, 'Professional Organization in Great Britain', *Industrial Relations*, October 1965; see also G. L. Millerson, *The Qualifying Associations* (Routledge, 1964).

not suffice to distinguish the main types of British trade unions, Clegg and his associates have suggested five groupings.[4] *General* unions are defined roughly according to the traditional classification. In preference to the old 'industrial union', which suggests the inclusion of all workers in a given industry and no one else, *single-industry* unions describe those that are confined to, or have their predominant interest in, a single industry. A rigid application of the criterion of apprenticeship would unduly narrow the definition of 'craft unions', and so the term *skilled* unions is preferred and includes those workers who acquire skill by promotion on the job. Craft unions which have changed the basis of their membership to include semi-skilled and unskilled workers constitute a fourth category of *ex-craft* unions. Finally, *white-collar* unions cater for clerical, supervisory, administrative and technical workers.

The question of democracy in trade union organization and practices has received considerable attention and is bound up with the problem of apathy of many members towards the running of their union's affairs. The degree of apathy varies among unions and low voting figures in elections for officers are often cited as evidence. An American study concludes that union participation may depend on the nature (1) of the individual, (2) of his social and primary groups, and (3) of the union organization.[5] Features influencing participation include respectively (1) class consciousness, the gregarious nature of particular individuals, and the intensity of association away from the workplace with fellow workers, (2) the extent of homogeneity of the fellow group members, and the physical nature and status of the job, and (3) the size of the union, its relative growth, and type of leaders.

Two main definitions of democracy have been used in the analysis of union politics: leadership responsiveness to membership opinion, and the institutionalization of opposition. Martin rejects both, and defines democracy in this context as the survival of faction.[6] He explains the survival of faction in terms of the

---

[4] H. A. Clegg *et al.*, *Trade Union Officers* (Oxford: Blackwell, 1961), p. 14f; for a consideration of the differences between 'open' (expansionist) and 'closed' (restrictionist) unions see H. A. Turner, *Trade Union Growth, Structure and Policy* (Allen & Unwin, 1962), p. 241f. The problem of classification is also discussed in J. Hughes, *Trade Union Structure and Government*, Research Paper 5, Royal Commission on Trade Unions and Employers' Associations (HMSO, 1967).

[5] M. M. Perline and V. R. Lorenz, 'Factors Influencing Member Participation in Trade Union Activities', *American Journal of Economics and Sociology*, October 1970.

[6] R. Martin, 'Union Democracy: An Explanatory Framework', *Sociology*, May 1968.

pressures which prevent union executives from destroying it. These include some fairly obvious factors such as a democratic political culture and a high level of membership participation, but also some less obvious correlates such as a low level of ownership concentration coupled with disagreement between predominantly friendly employers, and decentralized collective bargaining. Edelstein and Warner compared the pattern of opposition in British and American unions by means of a survey of the extent of opposition for top posts.[7] They concluded that the level of formal democracy, particularly in terms of the closeness of elections, is higher for British unions. On the other hand, American unions feature open, well-organized factions and a somewhat greater frequency of defeat of incumbents. The more sustained level of opposition in Britain seems to be largely due to the more limited powers of the top office, the various features surrounding the succession, and the method of electing the executive committee.

Another aspect of democracy in trade union organization is the vexed question of the 'closed shop'.[8] Broadly speaking, a closed shop means that a person cannot work in a particular job without being a union member. In 1964 it was estimated that about one worker in six was in a closed shop, and among trade unionists in manual occupations it was thought to be one in two. The aim in having 100% union membership is to ensure that the union bargains from a position of strength, that rates of pay agreed between the union and the management are not undercut by non-unionists, and that all workers benefiting from union negotiations subscribe to union funds. The Industrial Relations Act of 1971 prohibits closed shops (with a very few exceptions), but allows 'agency shops', i.e. where a worker who does not wish to be a union member must pay a contribution to the union equal to the subscription less optional extras or pay the same amount to a charity.

Workplace strategies

One of the most significant developments in trade unionism in recent years has been the growth of workplace bargaining and the increasing power of shop stewards. There are a number of reasons for this growth, but perhaps the key one is the role of informal organization in the industrial structure, as outlined in

[7] J. D. Edelstein and M. Warner, 'The Pattern of Opposition in British and American Unions', *Sociology*, May 1970.

[8] For a full account of this issue prior to the Industrial Relations Act see W. E. J. McCarthy, *The Closed Shop in Britain* (Oxford: Blackwell, 1964).

Chapter 9. In addition to whatever formal activities and practices occur, there are in most workplaces patterns of inter-personal relations over and above what is specified by the formal structure. One aspect of this is the way in which formal 'procedure' between management and unions for dealing with workers' grievances and claims is increasingly being supplemented by the informal activities of shop stewards.[9]

Shop stewards are trade union representatives at the place of work. Some union rule books make no mention of stewards, and even those that do are not always an accurate reflection of the workplace situation. It has been suggested that the power of stewards has increased because their functions and responsibilities have never been clearly defined. This undoubtedly facilitates the activities of stewards, but does not adequately explain why their increasing role in the industrial relations system has been largely accepted by other actors in the system. For the key to this we must look to the circumstances and motives of these other actors. As compared with taking a dispute 'through the procedure', there are advantages to both management and labour in settling it at workplace level. One result of involving higher levels is to increase the size of the staffs needed to process the grievances. From the union point of view, higher-level settlement increases the stability and binding power of the agreement and leaves less room for manoeuvre at local level.

The role of the shop steward has many features of sociological interest. He interacts with three sets of participants in the industrial relations system—his members (i.e. his fellow-workers), the full-time officers of his union, and members of management in the firm for which he works. His 'opposite number' on the management side is the foreman or first-line supervisor, and most of his management contacts are on this level. The role he plays is thus divided into three sectors, and his skill as a negotiator and mediator is tested by his ability to satisfy the different demands of the groups he deals with. To his members he is someone who speaks up for them to management and wins better pay or conditions for them; to his union he is someone who carries out union policy at the workplace; and to management he is (according to the attitude of the particular management members) someone who

[9] W. E. J. McCarthy and S. R. Parker, *Shop Stewards and Workshop Relations*, Research Paper 10, Royal Commission on Trade Unions and Employers' Associations (HMSO, 1968); see also J. F. B. Goodman and T. G. Whittingham, *Shop Stewards in British Industry* (McGraw-Hill, 1969), who also discuss the role of the 'informal work group leader' who may in some circumstances represent the views of workers against those of their steward.

is a troublemaker to be mastered or a responsible mediator between themselves and the ordinary workers.

The 'ideal type' of a steward would combine each of these role sectors into an integrated whole. He would manage to reconcile the conflicting role expectations which each of the three groups has of him. In practice, however, most stewards consider their obligations to be *primarily* towards only one of these groups. Thus Miller and Form have characterized three types of steward as job- or management-oriented, union-oriented and employee-oriented.[10] Parker and Bynner carried out a further analysis of the Donovan Royal Commission data and concluded that satisfaction with the industrial relations system at workplace level is not related to stewards' activism in the union or with militant attitudes, although activism and militancy overlap.[11] Also, the kind of *personal* satisfaction a steward gains from his union work appears to have virtually no bearing on his satisfaction with management–union relations, a conclusion that is difficult to reconcile with the 'human relations' view that keeping workers personally contented influences their co-operativeness. From factor analysis of stewards' attitudes and circumstances, it seems that management would be more likely to gain co-operation by being 'efficient' and 'reasonable' and by giving stewards a more extensive role to play.

INDUSTRIAL RELATIONS

The industrial relations system

The term 'industrial relations' is used in two ways: in the all-inclusive sense it refers to all the relationships between managers and employees within industry and in the community; in a more restricted sense it refers only to collective relations between unions and employers. But others are involved in industrial relations besides unions and employers; thus Barbash defines it as 'the area of study and practice concerned with the employment function in modern public and private enterprise; this function involves workers, unions, managers, government and the various "publics"'.[12] Flanders maintains that the industrial relations system is one of rules which appear in different guises: in legis-

[10] D. C. Miller and W. H. Form, *Industrial Sociology* (New York: Harper and Row, 1963), p. 393f.

[11] S. R. Parker and J. M. Bynner, 'Correlational Analysis of Data Obtained from a Survey of Shop Stewards', *Human Relations*, November 1970.

[12] J. Barbash, 'The Elements of Industrial Relations', *British Journal of Industrial Relations*, March 1964.

lation and statutory orders, in trade union regulations, collective agreements and arbitration awards, social conventions, managerial decisions, and accepted 'custom and practice'.[13]

Margerison takes issue with Flanders and suggests that industrial relations is a complex field of study which requires understanding at the behavioural, as well as institutional, level.[14] He points out that the emphasis tends to be put more on the consequences of industrial dispute than on its causes, and prefers a behavioural model for the analysis of the emergence of conflict in the plant social system. The key variables in this model are *objectives* (of the organization itself for survival, and of management and workers for control and material reward), *situation* (organization social system, technology, work task and job content), *interaction* (based on contracts of employment, organization and group structures, and role and authority relations), and *conflict* (to be analysed below).

In a critical review of the field, Blain and Gennard suggest that there are three competing industrial relations theories: the 'systems model', the 'Oxford approach', and an industrial sociology view.[15] The systems model is attributed primarily to Dunlop,[16] who, influenced by Parsons and Smelser, argued that an industrial relations system could be regarded as a sub-system of industrial society analogous with the economic sub-system (see Chapter 2). The Oxford approach, according to Blain and Gennard, takes industrial relations to be the study of the institutions of job regulation, which seems an unduly narrow position to attribute to, for example, many of the writers of the Donovan Commission research papers. The industrial sociology approach is said to reject the special emphasis given to rule determination by the other approaches and to favour the development of sociological models of conflict—which seems a fair assessment. Blain and Gennard, however, prefer the systems model, though they want it to take into account the process by which the rules of the system are determined.

Writing of industrial relations at workplace level, Parker and Scott maintain that theory and research have very largely gone

[13] A. Flanders, *Industrial Relations—What's Wrong with the System?* (Faber, 1965), p. 10.

[14] C. Margerison, 'What Do We Mean by Industrial Relations?', *British Journal of Industrial Relations*, July 1969.

[15] A. N. J. Blain and J. Gennard, 'Industrial Relations Theory—A Critical Review', *British Journal of Industrial Relations*, November 1970.

[16] J. T. Dunlop, *Industrial Relations Systems* (New York: Holt, Rinehart, 1958). For an application of this model see K. F. Walker, *Australian Industrial Relations Systems* (Cambridge, Mass.: Harvard University Press, 1970).

their own separate ways.[17] To guide future research, and to help develop testable hypotheses, they put forward a general model of variables involved in workplace industrial relations and a 'path' model of responses to proposals for changes in the state of the system. The general model consists of groups of variables between which certain causal relationships are posited: organization/ production variables, development of the industrial relations system, attitudes/behaviour of the parties, outside influences, and the quality of industrial relations. The path model seeks to study the system in action by tracing the steps following a proposal by either management or the unions to make a change affecting the workplace and those employed in it.

Even at a theoretical level it is difficult to remain dispassionate about industrial relations, because conflicting interest groups and policies are involved. Experts sympathetic to the problems of either management or trade unions naturally write from different perspectives, and their conclusions and proposals have to be judged accordingly. Thus Roberts questions the exercise of the right to strike and deplores the fact that 'agreements are . . . no longer looked upon as really binding upon the parties'.[18] Fox, however, takes a different view: 'Many instances of employees "dishonouring" agreements . . . can be explained by their never having "honoured" them in the first place, as a result of leaders failing to understand, or choosing to ignore, the process of winning consent'.[19] Such specific differences relate closely to a broader conception of industrial relations: a 'systems' view which sees the firm as an organic unity and stresses the underlying common interests of all parties to industrial relations, or an 'action' approach which sees the firm as a plural society and industrial relations as expressing the divergent interests of the parties involved. However, this is not to imply that taking either a systems or an action view of society predicts the adoption of a particular attitude to the nature of the industrial relations system or of the actions of individuals or groups within it. System theorists are obliged to 'recognize' industrial conflict behaviour, and action theorists seldom deny the meaningfulness of talking about an industrial relations system in at least some senses.

[17] S. R. Parker and M. H. Scott, 'Developing Models of Workplace Industrial Relations', *British Journal of Industrial Relations*, July 1971.

[18] B. C. Roberts (ed.), *Industrial Relations: Contemporary Problems and Perspectives* (Methuen, 1968), p. 24.

[19] A. Fox, *A Sociology of Work in Industry* (Collier-Macmillan, 1970), p. 151.

Productivity bargaining

An important development in the system of collective negotiations between management and unions has been the growth of productivity bargaining. At its simplest, this is an aspect of wage–work bargaining in which workers or their representatives accept changes in methods of working that contribute to higher productivity, in return for increases in earnings.[20] But there are implications which make this less simple in practice. It requires new ways of thinking and makes new demands on managers and supervisors; it is a challenge to some long-established and cherished trade union principles (including the raising of fundamental ideological issues about what should be the relations between employers and unions); and it represents a change in the socio-economic status of groups of employees that may disturb the relations between roles and rewards.

Towers and Whittingham point to additional features of productivity bargaining.[21] It is spreading rapidly throughout the economy and is changing the traditional system of collective bargaining. It is largely taking place at the level of the plant. And it is hoped that it will make a significant contribution towards an increase in the rate of growth of productivity in the economy as a whole. The early productivity agreements, of which the Esso Fawley is perhaps the classic case,[22] aimed at reducing or eradicating overtime, reducing levels of manning, and increasing flexibility between operatives and craftsmen and among craftsmen. These agreements were largely confined to capital-intensive, process industries such as oil and chemicals. However, successful productivity agreements have since been negotiated in labour-intensive, service industries like British Rail and the Post Office, and some of these have included attempts to achieve additional aims such as improved industrial relations and restructuring of jobs to give workers more involvement and satisfaction. The study by Cotgrove and his colleagues of a productivity agreement in a nylon spinning factory shows that it has increased operatives' overall happiness with the job, but

[20] W. W. Daniel, *Beyond the Wage-work Bargain* (PEP, 1970); see also S. Cotgrove *et al.*, *The Nylon Spinners* (Allen & Unwin, 1971), Chapter 1. For a more critical view see T. Topham, 'Productivity Bargaining', in K. Coates *et al.* (eds.), *Trade Union Register* (Merlin Press, 1969).

[21] B. Towers and T. G. Whittingham (eds.), *The New Bargainers : A Symposium on Productivity Bargaining* (Nottingham University Department of Adult Education, 1970).

[22] A. Flanders, *The Fawley Productivity Agreements* (Faber, 1964); for a summary see *Productivity Bargaining*, Research Paper 4, Royal Commission on Trade Unions and Employers' Associations (HMSO, 1967).

left them in little doubt that the company was the main beneficiary of the agreement.[23]

Industrial conflict

We are concerned here with the processes of development and resolution of strikes and other forms of industrial action (such as threats to strike, working to rule, 'go-slows' and overtime bans), and the circumstances in which these characteristically take place. In so far as we accept the 'plural society' or power-group interaction approach to the study of industrial relations, we may regard some form of conflict as endemic in industrial behaviour, and the question then becomes one of what constitute the form, circumstances and resolution of a particular instance.

An excellent analysis of industrial relations in coal-mining is given by Scott and his colleagues, in which strikes are treated in a more general context of industrial conflict.[24] Their findings contradict the commonly-held assumption that conflict in industry is necessarily harmful or always associated with inefficiency. They analyse conflict into two types and two ways in which it is expressed. *Basic* conflict exists when a group feels that its share in rewards is unjust from a long-term point of view; *procedural* conflict arises from disagreements about short-term variations in rewards and conditions of work. Also, conflict is expressed either in an organized or an unorganized way, the organized way being a group reaction to the vagaries of the industrial situation, and the unorganized way being a more personal reaction to its frustrations. The higher status groups more often engage in organized conflict, which requires a certain sense of group solidarity if it is to be carried through successfully.

Margerison makes a rather different analysis of types of conflict, which lends itself remarkably well to the threefold division of this book.[25] As with our divisions, he stresses that his types are not mutually exclusive. *Distributive* conflict relates to disputes that arise in the making or operation of the economic contract or wage-work bargain. This type of conflict may emerge from the market situation outside the firm, and the academic subject which diagnoses the problems involved is, in the main, economics. *Structural* conflict relates to the problems that emerge from the interactions within the formal structure of the organization. It is usually the result of failure to structure the organization properly —or failure to adapt its structure in times of change—to deal with

[23] Cotgrove, *op. cit.*, pp. 58, 131-2.
[24] W. H. Scott *et al.*, *Coal and Conflict* (Liverpool: University Press, 1963).
[25] Margerison, *op. cit.*

the role and authority problems of the organization. Industrial or organizational sociology specifically deals with this type of conflict. Finally, *human relations* conflict is at the role-person level—exemplified by a clash of personalities, or people with differing views disrupting social relations (not a trivial occurrence, since in the last resort all conflict is manifested at this level). This is the field of social psychology and micro sociology. These three types of conflict are typically resolved in different ways: distributive conflict by collective bargaining, structural by management agreeing to restructure the organization, and human relations by what are traditionally called leadership and 'man-management'.

Before turning to some further considerations in the causes of industrial conflict, we may briefly note a minor controversy concerning Britain's relative proneness to strikes. Turner has argued that the assumptions as to the frequency, character and costs of strikes in Britain, made in Labour and Conservative statements and the Donovan report, are highly dubious.[26] Because of differences in definition and reporting, international strike statistics are notoriously unreliable and, not surprisingly, McCarthy, as the Donovan research director, did not agree that its international comparison of strikes was unfair to Britain.[27] He added that Britain's strike problem takes two forms: '(1) A steady upward creep of small-scale unconstitutionalism which sometimes results in the creation of a strike-prone group in particular firms or plants. (2) The fact that sometimes unconstitutionalism results in the odd strike which causes a disproportionate amount of damage to the national economy and results in large numbers of workers who are not involved being laid off.' There is more room to disagree with the terminology than with the substance of those remarks.

Eldridge has outlined some of the factors making for high strike proneness: a single industry community, little occupational differentiation, geographical or social isolation of the group from the wider society, and high group cohesion.[28] To obtain a fuller picture of the causes of disputes one needs to take into account at least industrial differences, if not more local circumstances. Thus

[26] H. A. Turner, *Is Britain Really Strike-Prone?* (Cambridge University Press, 1969).

[27] W. E. J. McCarthy, 'The Nature of Britain's Strike Problem', *British Journal of Industrial Relations*, July 1970. International comparisons of working days lost, and other strike statistics, are conveniently summarized in A. F. Sillitoe, *Britain in Figures* (Penguin, 1971), pp. 114–21.

[28] J. E. T. Eldridge, *Industrial Disputes* (Routledge, 1968). Cf. A. Kornhauser et al. (eds.), *Industrial Conflict* (New York: McGraw-Hill, 1954).

Clack found that it was not (as is sometimes claimed) inter-union relations that caused strikes, but either the instability of employment or earnings or the wage structure and wage system.[29] Also, many workers felt that if satisfactory settlement of an issue could not be obtained at departmental level, there was a possibility that the issue might become distorted or merged with other issues at the higher levels of procedure. This helps to explain why 'unconstitutionalism' has increasingly been resorted to, and it points to the need for better and more acceptable procedures. Perhaps the best recent case-history of a strike is that written by Lane and Roberts about the Pilkington St Helens glassworks dispute.[30] Started through an error in wage calculation in one department leading to a spontaneous eruption from the shop floor, it brought out about 8,500 men for seven weeks in support of a big wage claim. The remoteness of the General and Municipal Workers' Union leaders from the shop floor undoubtedly played a part, but the exhilarated feeling of rebelling against the routine of factory life cannot be discounted: 'The way some of the men were talking it was as though they had done something big for the first time in their lives.'

INDUSTRIAL PARTICIPATION

Industrial democracy

The concept of industrial democracy embraces at one extreme the demand for 'workers' control' involving an economic and social revolution of ownership and management. At the other extreme it may be a somewhat grandiloquent description of quite modest steps to meet the growing demand of workers for more participation in the running of otherwise conventional enterprises. In between these extremes come the various 'experiments in industrial democracy'—short of revolution but more far-reaching than suggestion boxes and works committees—which have been made by certain enterprises. Whatever the merits and demerits of the movement for workers' control,[31] it has not been embraced by more than a small minority of workers in Britain, who generally have preferred to advance their interests through collective bargaining.

[29] G. Clack, *Industrial Relations in a British Car Factory* (Cambridge University Press, 1967), pp. 93–8; see also H. A. Turner *et al.*, *Labour Relations in the Motor Industry* (Allen & Unwin, 1967).

[30] T. Lane and K. Roberts, *Strike at Pilkingtons* (Fontana, 1971).

[31] The case in favour is stated in K. Coates and T. Topham (eds.), *Workers' Control* (Panther, 1970).

Flanders and his colleagues have studied the John Lewis Partnership (a large retail sales organization) and noted features of its ideology.[32] One is common ownership—not in the 'full communism' sense, but meaning that 'all who work permanently for the business are its owners and share the rewards of the enterprise'. Partners are remunerated 'according to the worth of their services to the success of the enterprise'. The Partnership looks upon itself as a community as well as a business and grants aid to its less fortunate members according to impersonal criteria. Managers are accountable for their decisions to the managed, but workers are not given the right to appoint their bosses, as this would prejudice the economic viability of the enterprise. The authors conclude that 'the ethos of the employment relationship for the non-managerial employees of the Partnership closely resembles that to be found in employing organizations of the usual kind. Although they may regard the Partnership as a "good" employer, their relationship with it remains a "calculative" rather than a "normative" one; except for a small minority it does not entail any firm commitment to the Partnership's ideology.'

Other experiments in industrial democracy have succeeded in making a greater break with conventional authority and role relationships in industry, without aiming at workers' control. One such is the Scott Bader Commonwealth, described by Blum as a 'quest for a new social order'.[33] Emery and Thorsrud have compared Norwegian experiments with those in Great Britain, West Germany and Yugoslavia.[34] Their general conclusion is that 'these systems seem to be valued by the workers as at least a gesture in the right direction, even though they might not seem to achieve much'.

Alternative forms of participation

If attachment to work is seen as more than merely instrumental to adequate income, and if there is some concern with the quality of working life, then employees' participation in decision-making may be valued as a step towards industrial democracy. It may be argued that, even though there are strong alienating tendencies in much modern industrial work, these can be significantly offset by

[32] A. Flanders et al., Experiment in Industrial Democracy (Faber, 1968), pp. 180-9.
[33] F. H. Blum, Work and Community (Routledge, 1968); see also the case study in participative management discussed in B. Shenfield, Company Boards (Allen & Unwin, 1971), Chapter 2.
[34] F. E. Emery and E. Thorsrud, Form and Content in Industrial Democracy (Tavistock, 1969).

'participation' which tends to transform the workers' definition of the work situation.[35] Some writers, however, take a more cautious view, particularly if the proposal is couched in the form of joint control of the firm by management and employees. Thus Ross finds this type of control theoretically justified in some form, but hardly representing any significant advance in the power and influence of employees beyond what is already available to them through collective bargaining.[36]

The basic dilemma facing those who wish to see a greater measure of democracy in industry is that, within the present structure of management authority and restricted aspirations of employees, there is really very little scope for it. As Robertson and Thomas remark, 'basic conflicts of interest must always make impossible the grandiloquent, participative parts so frequently wished upon the unions'.[37] Understandably, the unions view any commitment to employee representation on management boards with grave doubt, since, in the eyes of their members, such commitments prejudice their standing as the defender of employee interests. If employees come to define their interests as wider than just to maximize earnings, then the way is open for them either collectively to make further inroads into 'management prerogatives' via their unions or individually to take over some of the role content of managers themselves. Some of the newer forms of technology which give employees more autonomy and responsibility on the job, plus the growth of service and the decline of unskilled occupations, may aid this latter process.

[35] P. Blumberg, *Industrial Democracy: The Sociology of Participation* (Constable, 1968).
[36] N. S. Ross, *Constructive Conflict* (Edinburgh: Oliver and Boyd, 1969).
[37] N. Robertson and J. L. Thomas, *Trade Unions and Industrial Relations* (Business Books, 1968), p. 205.

The Labour Force and Mobility

IN this third and final part of the book we turn to an area which is sometimes described as the sociology of work and occupations. The essential concern is with the social roles which individuals play in the industrial structure or in specific types of work organization, and the implications that these roles have for them as persons. In this chapter some salient features of the labour force are briefly described, followed by a discussion of occupational roles and their correlates, and concluding with a review of aspects of occupational mobility and research findings concerning them.

THE LABOUR FORCE

The labour force consists of three categories of people: those in paid employment (full or part-time), those who are registered as available for work, and those who are available for work but not registered as such. American labour force statistics cover all three of these categories, but British statistics cover only the first two groups.

In Great Britain the labour force now consists of about 24 million persons out of a total population of about 56 million. The proportion of the labour force in the total population is important because the balance is made up of dependants who must be economically supported by the working population. Three factors are likely to result in a continuation of the falling proportion of working to dependant population: (1) a rising birth rate, (2) raising the school-leaving age to sixteen in 1972, and (3) a longer expectation of life in retirement.

One of the problems caused by an ageing population is the extent to which the community as a whole is willing to devote a larger proportion of its wealth to the growing group of 'non-producers'. One alternative is to provide employment, perhaps different from that done in the main part of working life, for those who have reached retiring age but are willing, and in some cases even eager, to continue working. Other consequences of an ageing labour force include its effect on incentives (the elderly are more concerned with security) and the possibilities of advancement for the younger.

Considerable changes have taken place during the last few decades in both the industrial and occupational distribution of the labour force. The industries which have employed increasing numbers of workers in recent years include miscellaneous services, and national and local government service. Those with decreasing numbers of employees include agriculture and fishing, mining and construction.[1] There has been an increasing proportion of employers and managers, professional employees and non-manual workers. Even in as short a period as one decade, the changes can be seen from the table below:[2]

Changes in proportions of selected socio-economic groups, 1961–71
(England and Wales %)

	1961	1971
Employers and managers	7·7	9·0
Professional employees	2·2	2·9
Non-manual workers	25·2	28·8
Manual workers	46·3	41·6
Agricultural workers	1·8	1·2
Other groups	16·8	16·5
	100·0	100·0

OCCUPATIONAL ROLES

The scope and pervasiveness of occupational roles are important aspects of the sociology of occupations. *Role* denotes the recognized part played by an individual in a social organization. The *scope* of an occupational role refers to the extent of the part that the incumbent plays in the work organization, while *pervasiveness*

[1] Decreasing numbers of employees are not necessarily associated with decreasing output; a smaller labour force may use more efficient methods and machines to raise output.
[2] Source: *Census 1971 England and Wales* (HMSO).

indicates its degree of penetration into other life-roles. The higher the status of an occupation, the more numerous and specific its role elements tend to be.[3] Thus only a few requirements for the position of floor sweeper are imposed, since this occupation involves only some limited, well-defined central elements and virtually no peripheral elements; whereas the position of an executive in a large company requires many more qualities than those of formal competence.

The pervasiveness of an occupational role bears no direct relation to its status. Some highly pervasive occupations, such as that of village policeman, carry relatively low status (though often high *prestige*) while less pervasive occupations, such as that of industrialist, are accorded high status. Banton spells out the difference between more and less pervasive occupational roles, though his example of blacksmith might be replaced by almost anyone who has a 'nine-to-five' job over which there is relatively lax social control: '. . . . blacksmith is a role which someone assumes for part of the day only; when he has finished work the incumbent is not expected to behave in any way different from people who are not blacksmiths'.[4] This role is contrasted with that of the policeman, who has obligations he is supposed never to lay aside. Being a policeman usually comes to affect a man's whole outlook on life.

Some occupational roles, because of the element of service to others that they involve, tend to pervade the rest of life. Social workers in general, and residential social workers in particular, may find it neither easy nor appropriate to stop being of service to others in their off-duty hours.[5] On the other hand, the navvies studied by Sykes showed a distinct reluctance to identify with their occupational role; none of them regarded themselves as permanent civil engineering workers but talked constantly of giving it up.[6]

CORRELATES OF OCCUPATIONAL MEMBERSHIP

For much evidence of correlates of occupational membership

---

[3] S. A. Weinstock, 'Role Elements: A Link Between Acculturation and Occupational Status', *British Journal of Sociology*, June 1963.

[4] M. Banton, *Roles: An Introduction to the Study of Social Relations* (Tavistock, 1965), p. 40.

[5] S. R. Parker, *The Future of Work and Leisure* (MacGibbon and Kee, 1971), Chapter 7.

[6] A. J. M. Sykes, 'Navvies: Their Social Relations', *Sociology*, May 1969; see also P. G. Hollowell, *The Lorry Driver* (Routledge, 1968), for an account of this occupational role and its effect on non-work life.

we have to rely on social class data rather than specifically occupational data. Even research on the latter is very limited in Britain, though findings from other countries suggest testable hypotheses. In Chicago in 1940 a person from the lowest economic class could expect to live five years less than average and nine years less than those in the highest economic class;[7] such differences are probably decreasing to the extent that primary poverty is diminished. Infant death rates in Britain have been shown to vary considerably according to the social class of the father: in 1958 the mortality ratio for infants of social class 5 fathers (unskilled) was nearly twice as high as for those of class 1 fathers (professional).[8]

Suicide rates are generally higher for white-collar and professional groups than for manual workers, but there are significant differences within these broad occupational groups that reflect particular types of work experience. Lonely occupations, such as domestic service and lodging-house keeping, have high suicide rates, while occupations which bring men into close contact with each other, such as miners and the clergy, have low suicide rates. Concerning mental health generally, American evidence shows that neurosis is concentrated in higher classes and psychosis in the lower, and that there are differences in diagnosis and methods of treatment between members of different classes with the same disorder.[9]

One of the more complex correlates of occupational membership is that of social conformity. High-status occupations include those giving personal freedom and a high degree of immunity from moral sanctions.[10] But occupations associated with 'sacred elements' or charged with social responsibility require their practitioners to function as models or examples. These two points mean that the strictest control over non-work behaviour tends to be found in occupations with important role-setting obligations, identification with sacred symbols, and relatively low status. Those occupations with least control over non-work behaviour tend to have high status and no involvement with sacred elements. Teaching is an example of relatively strict control over non-work behaviour, and advertising of relatively little control.

[7] E. V. Schneider, *Industrial Sociology* (New York: McGraw-Hill, 1969), p. 430.
[8] N. R. Butler and D. G. Banham, *Perinatal Mortality* (Edinburgh: Livingstone, 1963), p. 20.
[9] A. B. Hollingshead and F. Redlich, *Social Class and Mental Illness* (New York: Wiley, 1958).
[10] T. Caplow, *The Sociology of Work* (New York: McGraw-Hill, 1964), pp. 129–30.

OCCUPATIONAL MOBILITY

Occupational or labour mobility refers generally to the movement of workers. This movement can be of six types: (1) in or out of the labour force, (2) changes in the content of the job, (3) changes in the employer, (4) changes in the occupation or skills used, (5) changes in the industry or ends to which skills are put, and (6) changes in the geographical place of work.[11] Quite often one kind of change involves another. Occupational mobility is also sometimes used to describe a comparison of father's and son's occupation (inter-generational mobility) and in this sense it is an important factor in social mobility.

Surveys

In the post-war period there have been two large-scale British surveys of labour mobility. The first covered the period 1945–49 and involved over 5,000 men and women.[12] It was found that 28% of the men and 32% of the women had changed their employer at least once during this period; more young than old had changed their jobs, more manual than non-manual, and more unskilled than skilled. There were also differences in mobility rates among industries, for example, the rate was nearly twice as high in building as in miscellaneous services.

Over a lifetime men had made on average nearly four and women nearly three changes of occupation, industry, or location. Of the men's changes, roughly two were of occupation or industry within the same town, one was of occupation or industry involving a move, and one was geographical only (including those in the armed forces). Occupational changes were analysed according to whether or not they were within the same broad group of occupations: 61% of changes by those in professional or technical occupations were within that group, but only 30% of clerical workers' changes were within clerical work. Only 1% of operatives moved into professional or technical jobs, but 10% of the latter changed to the former. Most people changing their jobs went from one industry to another, though they often stayed within the same broad group. In short, workers appear to be more tied by their occupation than by the industry in which they work.

The second labour mobility survey was carried out in 1963,

[11] P. M. Hauser, 'Mobility in Labour Force Participation', in E. W. Bakke *et al.*, *Labour Mobility and Economic Opportunity* (New York: Technology Press, 1954), p. 11.

[12] G. Thomas, *Labour Mobility in Great Britain, 1945–1949* (Government Social Survey, 1949).

covering the previous ten years and involving a sample of nearly 20,000 men and women.[13] It was found that 57% of those who had been in the labour force in those ten years had remained in the same job, 19% had changed jobs once, and 11% twice in the period. About 1% had at least ten jobs in the ten years. Persons of managerial and executive status changed jobs less frequently than those in other occupational status groups. An analysis of reasons for leaving jobs showed that roughly one-fifth represented non-voluntary terminations or retirements, another fifth moved for better pay or prospects, and a similar proportion terminated through ill-health or changes in domestic responsibility.

The survey also enquired about the attitudes of employees to possible future movements for work purposes. Nearly half of the men and three-fifths of the women workers said that nothing would encourage them to move for a job. The factors that would have most influenced those who were prepared to consider moving were pay, promotion and job prospects, and the provision of good housing. Generally, the more highly qualified the informants were, the more willing they were to move. Just over half the sample thought it would be reasonably easy to get a suitable job without moving, but there is reason to believe that, with the increase in redundancy in recent years, this proportion would now be lower.

Measurement and interpretation

When occupational mobility is used in the sense of father-to-son changes, the father's occupation is usually cross-classified by the son's. For example, if 60% of the sons of professional fathers are professionals (40% mobile), while 20% of the sons of clerks are clerks (80% mobile), the latter are said to be twice as mobile as the former.[14] But this measure does not take into account the number of positions available in each occupational class. If, for example, there are three times more unskilled workers than professional then we should expect three times more mobility into unskilled work than into professional. Total mobility is the result of structural or availability factors plus personal or group factors. We must therefore ask whether movement within the occupational structure is more restricted for some groups than for others, since it is a question of share of opportunities.

Whether movements are measured in raw numbers, percent-

[13] A. I. Harris, *Labour Mobility in Great Britain, 1953–63* (Government Social Survey, 1966); see also summaries in *Ministry of Labour Gazette*, July 1966 and April 1967.
[14] N. Rogoff, *Recent Trends in Occupational Mobility* (Glencoe: Free Press, 1953), p. 29.

ages, or departures from standardized expectations, upward mobility exceeds that of downward mobility. This is partly because some of the occupational groups near the top of the status hierarchy (professional and white-collar) have expanded rapidly, whereas some of those near the bottom (agricultural and unskilled workers) have contracted. A second factor is that of differential fertility—the tendency of the wealthier to have fewer children. Because families of higher occupational status have generally had less than their proportionate share of children, room is left for others to rise into that status.

An important enquiry concerning occupational mobility was carried out in America by Blau and Duncan.[15] Using census and original survey data, they developed a path model of inter-generational mobility, the basic version of which is shown below:

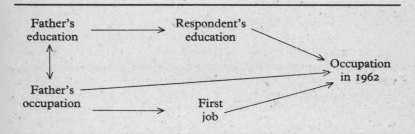

The model depicts the various influences on the status of a respondent's first job and on his occupation in 1962. The respondent's own educational attainment is most strongly correlated with the status of his first job, followed by father's occupation and (indirectly) by father's education. Also, occupational status in 1962 is influenced by respondent's education—more strongly than by the status of his first job. Further work is proceeding at Nuffield College in Britain on the dynamics of occupational mobility, comparable with the Blau and Duncan survey and designed to replicate the earlier British enquiry by Glass and his colleagues.[16]

We may briefly consider some further factors which influence intra-generational occupational mobility. The state of the labour market plays a big part. Voluntary movement is slight when job opportunities are few and when they are more plentiful

[15] P. M. Blau and O. D. Duncan, *The American Occupational Structure* (New York: Wiley, 1967), especially Chapter 5.
[16] D. V. Glass (ed.), *Social Mobility in Britain* (Routledge, 1954).

differentials in earnings and fringe benefits become more important in explaining mobility. Wilensky has noted the effect of type of employing organization.[17] Those in organizations with 'tall' hierarchies (affording careers with many stages) and with a high ratio of managers to managed are more likely to experience mobility than those in organizations with a long, prescribed training period. Broom and Smith have coined the term 'bridging occupation' to describe an occupation which provides, through work experience, the conditions and opportunities for movement from one to another.[18] Attributes of those in bridging occupations were found to be resocialization (redirection of the perspectives and aspirations of the occupant), independency, health and physical bearing, access to information or to individuals in influential or useful positions, and financial competence. Examples given of bridging occupations were servants, soldiers, school teachers, and those in occupations connected with mass communication and entertainment.

Parker has put forward the concept of 'retrospective bridging' in connection with those occupations in which experience of other kinds of work is relatively frequent and highly valued.[19] Using survey data, three different types of occupation were examined for the degree to which their members had been occupationally mobile. Bank workers were shown to have had little retrospective mobility compared with youth employment and child care officers. The past occupations of the latter were mainly those involving contact with clients or customers; bank work requires fewer social or personal skills and a varied occupational history is no advantage.

Redundancy

Redundancy—officially defined as occurring when the 'reason for dismissal is that the employer's needs for employees to do work of a particular kind have diminished or ceased'—has been increasing in recent years. The end of the post-war sellers' market, inflation, and the uncertain outlook for British industry as a whole have combined to make increasing numbers of employers go out of business or reduce costs by making part of their labour force redundant. In 1965 the Government introduced the Redundancy

[17] H. L. Wilensky, 'Work, Careers and Social Integration', *International Social Science Journal*, No. 4, 1960.

[18] L. Broom and J. H. Smith, 'Bridging Occupations', *British Journal of Sociology*, December 1963.

[19] S. R. Parker, 'Retrospective "Bridging" of Three Occupational Groups', *Sociology*, January 1967.

Payments Act, which provided for a statutory payment of up to £1,200 to employees made redundant. The sociological significance of this Act is that it recognizes that employees in effect accumulate 'property' rights in a job and deserve to be compensated if they lose it through no fault of their own. The payments, based on earnings, age and length of service (with a minimum qualifying period of two years) are met partly by the particular employers involved and partly by a fund financed by the contributions of all employers. By 1971 the annual rate at which employees were made redundant with a statutory payment had reached 400,000, though by 1974 the annual rate had declined to about half that figure.

A survey carried out in 1969 showed that people who lost their jobs through redundancy generally fared worse than those who changed jobs for other reasons.[20] Five out of six redundant employees were able to get other jobs within a year of redundancy, but less than half of those aged 60–64 were able to do so. People who did find post-redundancy employment tended to lose rather than gain in the skill level of their job, the income from it, pension rights, fringe benefits and job satisfaction. It is perhaps some consolation that the largest statutory payments were generally shown to have gone to those who had suffered the greatest losses as a result of redundancy.

Although strictly more relevant to an analysis of industrial organizations than of roles, the findings of the above survey concerning causes of redundancy are worth noting. The most frequent causes were 'economic' (chiefly fall in product demand) and 'technological' (reorganized work methods). These may respectively be regarded as externally caused and internally caused. The latter situations were found to be correlated with steps taken in advance to cope with the impact of redundancy, particularly attempts to minimize its effects on the employees involved (such as offering them retraining or attempting to place them with other employers). The externally-caused redundancies, on the other hand, were associated with structural features of the establishment, such as a low proportion of female workers, unionization, and a large number of employees.

[20] S. R. Parker et al., *Effects of the Redundancy Payments Act* (HMSO, 1971).

CHAPTER 13

The Subjective Experience of Work

AFTER considering some of the objective features of occupational membership and roles, we now turn to more subjective aspects of occupational experience. There are a number of concepts that are relevant here, and our first task is to try to define them in relation to each other and to see to what extent different terms are used in the same or very similar senses. There are two broad groups of concepts: those relating to the evaluation of work as a social activity or institution, and those relating to the subjective experience of particular work roles.

The first group consists of two concepts, ideology and value. A work *ideology* is held by the members of a society generally or by a particular social group and refers to a clustering of lower-order concepts such as values, attitudes, beliefs and opinions. It applies to those concepts and rules that function to maintain or challenge some part of the social order and that also serve to allay fears and create hopes.[1] Sometimes the terms 'ethos' and 'image of society' are used to denote something very similar to ideology. Work *values* are more specific 'conceptions of the desirable'[2] by which a particular society or group judges features of work to be good or bad. The differences between these two concepts should become clear as we examine research involving them in the sections below.

The group of concepts referring to the subjective experience of work roles includes, from the more general to the less: attitudes (or orientation), involvement, motivation, and satisfaction. There is a link between attitudes and values in that a work *attitude*

---

[1] J. Plamenatz, *Man and Society*, vol. 2 (Longmans, 1963), pp. 344-5.
[2] C. Kluckhohn, 'Values and Value-Orientations in the Theory of Action', in T. Parsons and E. Shils, *Toward a General Theory of Action* (Cambridge, Mass.: Harvard University Press, 1951), p. 422.

describes the general approach that a person has to his work as a result of accepting or rejecting certain values of his society or group. Work *involvement* refers to a special class of attitudes and signifies the degree to which a person is identified psychologically with his work or the importance of work in his total self-image. The meaning of work to a person is another way of indicating the quality of his involvement in it. *Motivation* usually refers to a specific job or narrow range of jobs rather than to work in general, and constitutes the factors that pull people towards achieving certain goals through the work. Finally, *satisfaction*, which is also normally job-specific, is a function of the discrepancy between what a worker expects, or thinks he should get, and what he actually experiences in the work situation.

WORK IDEOLOGY

It has been suggested that the post-war period has seen an 'end of ideology'—a drying-up of radicalism, and a turning of concern towards culture and status rather than politics.[3] Though by no means free from ambiguity, ideology in one sense denotes a coherent and long-term system of beliefs by which to guide our short-term actions and considerations. Thus to claim an end of ideology may be to claim either that we have arrived at a consensus about social goals or that we have lost interest in them. There is, however, another view. According to Fox, ideology is a resource in the struggle for power, since it shapes the ways in which men perceive, think, feel, and act.[4] In the world of work this is to say that there are *competing* ideologies, even though one of these may be dominant in a given context. Specifically, we may examine the extent to which management and labour have developed different or complementary ideologies related to work.

Bendix has shown that a 'managerial ideology' has developed that serves to justify the power of management in terms of basic cultural values; further, this ideology characterizes not just the business community but virtually the total American society.[5] The same may be said of British society. Management apologists seek to propagate an ideology that justifies management

[3] Daniel Bell, *The End of Ideology* (New York: Collier, 1961); see also the discussion of this in O. E. Klapp, *Collective Search for Identity* (New York: Holt, Rinehart, 1969).

[4] A. Fox, *A Sociology of Work in Industry* (Collier-Macmillan, 1971), pp. 124–32; see also J. Child, *The Business Enterprise in Modern Industrial Society* (Collier-Macmillan, 1969), pp. 47–8.

[5] R. Bendix, *Work and Authority in Industry* (New York: Harper and Row, 1963).

behaviour, legitimizes its rule, and evokes loyalty and commitment on the part of lower as well as higher participants. As Fox remarks, this ideology consists of assorted notions to suit varying exigencies, sometimes quite incompatible with each other. Thus what are described as 'incentives' for managers become 'bribes' when they have to be offered to wage-earners. But in general managerial ideology stresses a unitary conception of the organization. It is at once a method by which managers reassure themselves that a basic harmony exists that is opposed only by a misguided or malicious minority; an instrument to persuade their employees and the public at large that there is such a harmony; and a technique of seeking legitimation of their authority.

Trade unions and other employee associations also have their ideologies, though these tend to be more variable than those of management. At one extreme, some white-collar staff associations have an ideology virtually indistinguishable from that of management, stressing the validity and desirability of collaboration.[6] At the other extreme, some unions pursue militant policies based on an ideology of opposition and challenge to management, appealing to the solidarity of all workers and ultimately the brotherhood of man. Even in these cases, however, there is at the level of the union as an organization an ideological commitment to acceptance of the existing basic system of control.

Ideologies are mainly apparent at the level of large collectivities or whole societies, but may also be a feature of workers in a particular occupation. Long-established crafts, such as the compositors studied by Cannon,[7] tend to develop their own radical ideologies as part of a sense of occupational community. By contrast, Silverman has suggested that there is a relationship between the ideologies of groups of clerical workers and the type of organization for which they work.[8] In particular, he found that clerks in contact with manual workers were more likely to emphasize the social distance between white-collar and manual workers than were those not in contact. He explained this by the greater status-consciousness of the group in contact, brought about by a face-to-face view of diminishing differentials that conflicted with their aspiration to management positions.

[6] This is evident in the case of employee associations including the staff of industrial relations departments in large organizations, whose job is to deal with the grievances and claims of workers.

[7] I. C. Cannon, 'Ideology and Occupational Community: a Study of Compositors', *Sociology*, May, 1967.

[8] D. Silverman, 'Clerical Ideologies: a Research Note', *British Journal of Sociology*, September 1968.

WORK VALUES

Much of the research on work values has been concerned with the ways in which they are internalized during the process of occupational choice and training. One of the most comprehensive and theoretically enlightened studies is that of Rosenberg and his associates.[9] They gathered data on a nationwide basis of American students' preferences, expectations and aspirations in the work sphere. In general, students fell into three groups: those who ask what rewards they will get from their work; those who ask whether it will be a challenging, creative experience; and those who ask whether they will enjoy working with the people. Students planning to enter different occupations exhibited these values in varying proportions; for example, 'people-oriented' values were most strongly expressed by students planning to enter social work, medicine, social science and personnel work. Thus the relationship between occupational values and the nature of the work suggests that what the student wants from his work delimits and channels the range of occupations in which he might become interested. Several other investigators have examined the relationship between values and prospective careers, including the development of identification with an occupation.[10]

Moving to the level of the occupational world itself, Lyman compared the two broad groups of white-collar and blue-collar workers for differences in values attached to work.[11] She concluded that the former emphasized the nature of the work itself and freedom, and the latter the physically easy nature of the work, the economic rewards, conditions of work and cleanliness. These differences were not a function of differences in job satisfaction, for when satisfaction was held constant a pattern of different reasons for liking or disliking jobs was found. However, she noted the difficulty that the results might be open to other interpretations than value differences, for example, differences in what is taken for granted.

An example of different value orientations of two groups of employees doing roughly the same kind of tasks is given by Boggs.[12] Laboratory workers were divided into professionals and technicians, largely on the basis of education and prestige. It

---

[9] M. Rosenberg et al., *Occupations and Values* (Glencoe: Free Press, 1957).

[10] See for example S. Cotgrove and S. Box, *Science, Industry and Society* (Allen & Unwin, 1970).

[11] E. Lyman, 'Occupational Differences and Values Attached to Work', *American Journal of Sociology*, January 1956.

[12] S. T. Boggs, 'The Values of Laboratory Workers', *Human Organization*, Fall 1963.

was found that the professionals were far more likely to say that the kind of work they did was the most important thing about a life's work, while the technicians more often said that security or pay was the most important thing. One explanation of this difference in values is that the professionals expected to participate more fully in all phases of their work and were more often rewarded socially for doing so.

WORK ATTITUDES

Work attitudes describe the general approach that people take to their work as a result of having certain values. In this context the term 'orientation' means much the same as attitude, that is, a readiness to respond to aspects of work in terms of the values held. There have been many studies of the attitudes of people in various occupations and work situations. The findings of such studies may be grouped according to a small number of significant variables. The manual–non-manual categories, levels of skill, and age groups are obvious examples, though work situation variables such as degree of autonomy and social interaction are also important. To illustrate briefly some consequences of these variables for work attitudes we may select four groups of occupations which together account for a large proportion of the labour force: professionals, clerks, skilled craftsmen, and semi-skilled factory workers.

Caplow notes a number of features of professional work that combine to produce typical attitudes.[13] These features are: the distinction drawn between co-professionals and laymen, the concentration of interest which marks the professional career, the long period of training, and informal association outside working hours. The professional attitude to work is often contrasted with the bureaucratic attitude. The former is characteristic of the 'cosmopolitan', who tends to have a relatively low loyalty to his employing organization, a high commitment to his role skills and an 'outgroup' reference, while the bureaucrat typically shows high loyalty to his employing organization, low commitment to role skills and an 'ingroup' reference.[14]

The work attitudes of clerks reflect their varied work situations and social class affiliations. As Lockwood has shown, the older, more paternalistic work relations and environment of the clerk

---

[13] T. Caplow, *The Sociology of Work* (Minneapolis: University of Minnesota Press, 1954), p. 131f.
[14] A. W. Gouldner, 'Cosmopolitans and Locals', *Administrative Science Quarterly*, December 1957.

precluded any sense of identification with other types of worker, and led to individualistic aspirations to advancement akin to those of professionals.[15] But as office units have become larger and working relationships and techniques more impersonal and standardized—in short, more like those of the factory—group feeling, collective action and a 'trade union' attitude to earnings and working conditions have developed among clerks.

As a representative of skilled craft occupations we may take the printer. Studies in both Britain and America have described the nature of the 'occupational community' in which printers tend to live. Lipset and his associates show that intrinsic interest in the craft tends to promote a high degree of participation in the work organization and particularly in union activities.[16] The members of occupational communities see themselves in terms of their occupational role and their reference group is composed of other members of the occupational community. Salaman suggests that these attitudes are related to involvement in the work tasks (see below), marginal status and the inclusiveness of the work or organizational situation.[17]

The fourth group whose attitudes we may consider are semi-skilled factory workers. Car assembly workers have been the subject of several studies in America.[18] A much discussed enquiry in Britain by Goldthorpe and his colleagues broadly confirms the American findings that the car worker is typically alienated from his work, attached to his job only as a means of earning comparatively high wages, and is in some senses a prototype of the 'new working class'.[19] But they go on to develop a theoretical explanation of the orientation to work of these employees. They criticize both the 'human relations' school and the 'technological implications' approach: the former for supposing that men seek from their work not only money but also approval, recognition, and so on; and the latter for claiming that assembly-line technology generates more conflict between workers and their supervisors or managers than other technologies. Instead, they point to the

[15] D. Lockwood, *The Blackcoated Worker* (Allen & Unwin, 1958).

[16] S. M. Lipset *et al.*, *Union Democracy* (Glencoe: Free Press, 1956); see also Cannon, *op. cit.*

[17] G. Salaman, 'Some Sociological Determinants of Occupational Communities', *Sociological Review*, February 1971.

[18] R. Blauner, *Alienation and Freedom* (Chicago University Press, 1964); E. Chinoy, *Automobile Workers and the American Dream* (New York: Doubleday, 1955); A. Kornhauser, *Mental Health of the Industrial Worker* (New York: Wiley, 1965).

[19] J. H. Goldthorpe *et al.*, *The Affluent Worker: Industrial Attitudes and Behaviour* (Cambridge University Press, 1968).

significance of the wants and expectations that men *bring* to their work, and suggest that this prior 'orientation' shapes the attitudinal and behavioural patterns of their working lives as a whole. In the cases they studied the orientation to work was clearly instrumental and hence, they argued, the absence of such features of employment as solidary work groups or employee-centred supervision was unlikely to produce any marked degree of frustration or discontent.[20]

Goldthorpe and his colleagues maintain a *sociological* view of orientation to work, that is, they see it as socially generated and sustained. But there is also a *psychological* view, as expressed by Darley and Hagenah, who claim that the individual's occupational interests are well determined before job experience and that people of certain personality, perceptual habits, and value types characteristically seek out occupations that permit the free play of these behaviours.[21] On the other hand, Kohn and Schooler draw conclusions from their survey that are closer to Daniel's criticism of orientation.[22] They see occupational experiences as permeating men's views, not only of work and of their role in work, but also of the world and of self. They distinguish between conditions of work that facilitate intrinsic interest in the job and those that limit men's view of the job primarily to the extrinsic benefits it provides.

While not wishing to underestimate the role either of psychological differences or social factors in prior orientations to work, we may adduce one further piece of evidence in support of the independent effect of work situation variables on attitudes. Lieberman noted the effect of role changes on attitudes.[23] Workers who were made foremen became more favourable to management (though if demoted they reverted to worker attitudes), while those who were made shop stewards became more favourable to the union.

WORK INVOLVEMENT

We commonly speak of someone as 'involved' in his work if he makes a considerable emotional investment in it—if it 'means a lot to him'. But involvement in that sense is only quantitative,

[20] See Chapter 9 under 'Orientation to Work' for a critical discussion of the Goldthorpe thesis.

[21] J. G. Darley and B. Hagenah, 'The Meaning of Work and Jobs', in B. Hopson and J. Hayes, *The Theory and Practice of Vocational Guidance* (Oxford: Pergamon Press, 1968).

[22] M. L. Kohn and C. Schooler, 'Class, Occupation, and Orientation', *American Sociological Review*, October 1969.

[23] S. Lieberman, 'The Effects of Change in Roles on the Attitudes of Role Occupants', *Human Relations*, November 1956.

and says nothing about possible different *types*. Involvement may be seen to have three aspects: the meaning that is attached to work, the feeling of identification with or alienation from work, and the degree to which work is a central life interest. We shall consider each of these aspects in turn.

A number of studies have sought to define various meanings of work typically held by people in different occupations or work situations. Weiss and Kahn found that over three-fourths of respondents defined work either as activity which was necessary though not enjoyed, or as activity which was scheduled or paid for.[24] The first definition was associated with occupations that permit some autonomy (such as professionals and salespeople), and the second with occupations affording neither autonomy nor social standing (such as factory workers and labourers).

Friedmann and Havighurst compared the meaning of work to five occupational groups.[25] The workers of lower skill and socio-economic status were more likely to see their work as having no other meaning than that of earning money. Coalminers had a more personal sense than steelworkers of being pitted against their environment, and expressed feelings of accomplishment and pride at having conquered it. Skilled craftsmen showed a very high degree of emphasis on work as a source of self-respect and the respect of others. Salespeople attached many extra-economic meanings to their work, and even routine and association with others become meaningful life-experiences for them. Finally, the physicians were found to stress most the public service aspects of their jobs.

The method used by Morse and Weiss to study the meaning of work was to ask questions on the hypothesis that the economic necessity for their informants to work was removed.[26] They concluded that to those in middle-class occupations work means having something interesting to do, having a chance to accomplish things, and to contribute. By contrast, those in working-class occupations view work as synonymous with activity. These differences in work meanings correspond to differences in the content of the jobs. The content of professional, managerial and sales jobs concerns symbols and the handling of 'cases', and so a life without such work would be less purposeful, stimulating and

[24] R. S. Weiss and R. L. Kahn, 'Definitions of Work and Occupations', *Social Problems*, Fall 1960.

[25] E. A. Friedmann and R. J. Havighurst, *The Meaning of Work and Retirement* (Chicago University Press, 1954), pp. 3–5, 173–8.

[26] N. Morse and R. Weiss, 'The Function and Meaning of Work and the Job', *American Sociological Review*, April 1955.

challenging. Working-class occupations emphasize working with tools and machines, and the individual is oriented to the effort rather than to the end—life without work would mean life without anything to do.

The theme of alienation from work has been widely used to describe the disengagement of self from the occupational role. Frustrated by the lack of meaning in the tasks allotted to him and by his impersonal role in the work organization, the alienated worker is said to turn to non-work life for values and identity: 'I only work here, but if you want to know me as I really am, come to my home and meet my family.'[27] Alienation can also take subtler forms among professionals and executives, for whom it may be fashionable to be cynical about one's work but quite 'satisfied' with one's job. Experience of alienation is not confined to a few special occupations, though it tends to be associated with certain types of work situation. In large-scale bureaucracies it is apparent in the administration of men as if they were things.[28] In an automated factory or office it takes the form of increasing the number of people who deal with the world through abstractions.

An important contribution to understanding the nature and correlates of alienation from work has been made by Blauner.[29] In making a comparative analysis of four types of work situation he shows that alienation is a function of the type of industry in which people work. He analyses the dimensions of alienation as *powerlessness* (inability to control the work process), *meaninglessness* (inability to develop a sense of purpose connecting the job to the overall productive process), *isolation* (inability to belong to integrated industrial communities), and *self-estrangement* (failure to become involved in the activity of work as a mode of self-expression). Four types of industry are compared: the general picture is of a relative lack of alienation in craft printing, an increase in machine textiles, a further increase in the assembly-line automobile industry, but a return to something like the printing level in the automated chemical industry.

On the basis of his own research in a Swedish community, Seeman has questioned the validity of some of the wider claims made concerning alienation.[30] He found little evidence that

[27] P. L. Berger, 'Some General Observations on the Problem of Work', in P. L. Berger (ed.), *The Human Shape of Work* (New York: Macmillan, 1964), p. 217.

[28] E. Fromm, 'Freedom in the Work Situation', in M. Harrington and P. Jacobs, *Labor in a Free Society* (University of California Press, 1959).

[29] R. Blauner, *op. cit.*

[30] M. Seeman, 'On the Personal Consequences of Alienation in Work', *American Sociological Review*, April 1967.

alienated work, in the sense of work that is unrewarding in its own right, has the generalized consequences often imputed to it. The alienated worker is not more hostile to ethnic minorities, less knowledgeable and engaged in political matters, less sanguine about or interested in the possibility of exercising control over socio-political events, more status minded or more anomic. Seeman stresses that cross-cultural validation of these findings is essential, since Swedish society is different in many respects from other industrial societies. He also calls for more study of the social-psychological subtleties of the work process and of what it really means to talk about intrinsically rewarding activities, at work or elsewhere—a call that is partly answered by the excellent case studies reported by Fraser.[31]

A concept allied to, but in a sense the opposite of, alienation is that of *central life interest*. Following Dubin, this refers to a significant area of social experience.[32] Assuming that social participation in a sphere may be necessary but not important to an individual, Dubin classified replies by industrial workers to a series of three-choice questions as job-oriented, non-job-oriented, or indifferent. The results showed that by a margin of three to one work was not in general a central life interest for industrial workers. Orzack gave an amended version of Dubin's schedule to a sample of professional nurses, and his results confirmed the prediction that they would be much more oriented to work as a central life interest than industrial workers.[33] Parker also put 'central life interest' questions to bank employees, youth employment and child care officers, with the result that the first group emerged as substantially more non-work oriented than the other two.[34] The difference in central life interest was found to be associated with other work attitudes and with various work situation factors.

THE MOTIVATION TO WORK

There is a link between this section and the next on work satisfaction, in that the factors which motivate a person to work may be regarded as prospective 'satisfiers'. A good deal of research

[31] R. Fraser (ed.), *Work: Twenty Personal Accounts* (Penguin, 1968), vol. 2, 1969.
[32] R. Dubin, 'Industrial Workers' Worlds', *Social Problems*, January 1956.
[33] L. Orzack, 'Work as a "Central Life Interest" of Professionals', *Social Problems*, Fall 1959.
[34] S. R. Parker, *The Future of Work and Leisure* (MacGibbon and Kee, 1971), Chapter 7.

has been carried out by industrial psychologists on motives and incentives. Instead of trying to summarize these studies here,[35] we shall draw attention to perhaps the best known, most extensively applied, and most frequently criticized theory—that of Herzberg and his associates.[36] Using samples of engineers and accountants, they showed that factors which act as 'satisfiers' (and which have a definite motivational character) are different from those which prevent dissatisfaction (the 'hygiene' factors). Satisfied workers stressed achievement, recognition, the work itself, responsibility and advancement. Dissatisfied workers complained about company policy and administration, supervision, salary, interpersonal relations and working conditions.

As an example of an application of the Herzberg theory we may take the recent research carried out by Cotgrove and his colleagues into the work experiences of men in a nylon spinning factory.[37] The theory itself has been very thoroughly and critically evaluated by Wall and Stephenson.[38] Although their own research findings show the evidence for the two-factor theory to be largely a function of the 'need for social approval', they vindicate the policy of job enrichment as likely to promote satisfaction *and* allay dissatisfaction.

WORK SATISFACTION

There have been several hundred studies of job or work satisfaction and it is not possible to do more here than to review some of their main conclusions and to draw attention to some of their limitations.[39] Data have been obtained in a number of different ways. The most usual is simply to enquire of the informant whether and in what way he finds his present job satisfying. Sometimes the question 'in what way?' is asked in an open form, and sometimes the informant is presented with a list of factors from which to choose or to rank in order. Another method is to

[35] A summary is given in V. H. Vroom, *Work and Motivation* (New York: Wiley, 1964).

[36] F. Herzberg *et al.*, *The Motivation to Work* (New York: Wiley, 1959); F. Herzberg, *Work and the Nature of Man* (Staples Press, 1968).

[37] S. Cotgrove *et al.*, *The Nylon Spinners* (Allen & Unwin, 1971).

[38] T. D. Wall and G. M. Stephenson, 'Herzberg's Two-Factor Theory of Job Attitudes', *Industrial Relations Journal*, December 1970.

[39] This section is based on S. R. Parker, 'Work Satisfaction: A Review of the Literature', Governmental Social Survey paper M115, where details of sources are given. For a review including more recent sources see J. P. Robinson *et al.*, *Measures of Occupational Attitudes and Occupational Characteristics* (Ann Arbor, Mich.: Institute for Social Research, 1969).

ask what makes a job good or bad. A more sophisticated approach is first to posit certain needs in relation to work and then to enquire about the degree to which these are actually satisfied.

Many occupations have been the subject of work satisfaction studies, though factory and office work have predominated. Among skilled factory workers and craftsmen intrinsic satisfaction with the work itself is frequently found, especially when the job involves completion of a whole project. Assembly-line workers attach more importance to being able to control to some extent the pace and methods of their work. Variety of operations is a source of satisfaction to both factory and office workers, and among the latter the friendliness of the working group is often mentioned (particularly by females). In comparing proportions of satisfied workers in different occupations there seem to be separate scales for manual and non-manual jobs, with more satisfaction found at the higher levels of skill in each group. Professional workers are most satisfied, and semi-skilled and unskilled manual workers least satisfied.

Of 'special situation' factors that influence satisfaction, social interaction seems to be most important. Autonomy in the work situation—freedom to make decisions and take responsibilities—is positively related to satisfaction. If three individuals are engaged on the same work with mates doing a better, worse, or the same job, the first is likely to show least job enjoyment. Permissive supervision and leadership, and being consulted in advance about changes in work processes, are conducive to satisfaction. In general, jobs which involve dealing with people provide more satisfaction than those which do not.

Satisfaction is correlated with certain personal attributes. Women are generally more satisfied with their work than men, even when their jobs are lower in authority position, status and income. Satisfaction generally increases with age, although there is a tendency for the young to find this in intrinsic aspects of the work and the old to find it in the social and technical environment. Higher social class and status are related to satisfaction but, among those doing the same kind of work, better education is associated with lower satisfaction. Insecurity in a job, even when accompanied by good objective conditions, adversely affects satisfaction. The data on the relation of satisfaction to productivity are ambiguous: some studies have found a positive relationship, some a negative, and some no relationship.

In evaluating the conclusions of the various work satisfaction studies certain methodological and other criticisms need to be taken into account. Figures of general satisfaction with a job tell us very little, since we do not know what the questions mean to the people who answer them. The frame of reference of questions is often very limited, so that expressions of satisfaction are narrow and made without consciousness of possible alternatives. Also, we must differentiate between what people consciously think about their satisfaction and what they may feel unconsciously. The tendency to repress dissatisfaction is strongly supported by the widespread feeling that not to be satisfied is an admission of failure.

CHAPTER 14

Work and Leisure

THE relation between work and leisure has three dimensions, corresponding to the three parts of this book. At the institution-system level there is the relation between the institutions of work and of leisure; at the organization-role level we have the internal structure of work organizations and leisure organizations; and at the role-person level the focus is on the ways in which the working and leisure parts of individuals' lives affect each other. Most of this chapter will be devoted to the last of these three interests. This is a reflection partly of a deliberate restriction of a wide subject, and partly of the fact that more empirical research has been carried out in this area than in the other two areas. We shall first discuss some definitions and conceptual problems of work and leisure, then the data on the allocation of time to these two spheres, then the variables which affect the nature of their relationship, and finally we shall review the progress that has been made towards a theory of work and leisure.

THE NATURE OF WORK AND LEISURE

Although we can make certain statements about the nature of work and leisure separately, they have full sociological meaning only in relation to each other. Work is an activity that is carried on under conditions in which there are normally demands with respect to time and place and in which effort is directed to the production of goods and services. In leisure-time activities the demands are self-imposed; there is some feeling of freedom and normally a contrast to the external controls of time, space and production imposed in the work situation. For a minority of persons their work is to some extent also their leisure, or perhaps they do not find it meaningful to divide their lives into these two spheres. But the fact remains that for most people in contemporary industrial society leisure is quite clearly demarcated from work.

If work is a social demand and leisure a kind of individual demand, the same holds true for contributions. Work contributes something which others are willing to pay for (or for which others would have to be paid if one did not do it oneself), while leisure is concerned with contributing to the satisfaction of self.[1] Leisure may be regarded as an end, distinct from work as a means, provided that we make the exceptions that leisure is sometimes seen as a means to better work and that certain types of work may be valued for their own sakes. A social ethic may, in fact, be based either on work or leisure or an integration of the two. The movement that has taken place from a work-based Protestant ethic to a more leisure-based ethic does not mean that the former now exercises no influence. There is still a widespread belief that leisure is something that has to be earned and re-earned, except for the very old.[2]

It has been assumed so far that all life space, that is, activities or ways of spending time that people have, can be classified as either work or leisure. But important differences exist *within* as well as between the categories of work and leisure that make a closer analysis necessary. On the side of work, there is time actually spent on the job, and a fringe area that is defined according to one's conception of how far the domain of work extends.

DeGrazia calls this fringe area 'work-related time', meaning time spent in order to appear at work presentably (travelling to work or grooming oneself for work) or in doing things that one would not ordinarily do if it were not for work, like a husband doing a share of his working wife's housework.[3] On the side of leisure, Dumazedier has proposed the sub-category of *semi-leisure* to describe 'activities which, from the point of view of the individual, arise in the first place from leisure, but which represent in differing degrees the character of obligations',[4] The obligations are usually to other people, but may be to non-human objects such as pets or homes or gardens.

It has been suggested that free time is simply a space of time, while leisure is an activity or 'state of being'.[5] But this contrast is

[1] G. Soule, *Time for Living* (New York: Viking Press, 1955), p. 124.
[2] M. Mead, 'The Pattern of Leisure in Contemporary American Culture', *Daedalus*, September 1957.
[3] S. DeGrazia, *Of Time, Work and Leisure* (New York: Twentieth Century Fund, 1962), p. 246.
[4] J. Dumazedier, *Toward a Society of Leisure* (Collier-Macmillan, 1967).
[5] DeGrazia, *op. cit.*

not confined to the area of non-work—it applies also in the work sphere. The two worlds of time and activity are not the domains of work and leisure respectively: both are *dimensions* of work *and* leisure. Unless this two-dimensional property of work and leisure is appreciated, it is impossible to understand that work (or leisure) is a quality of activity that only problematically and not necessarily takes place within a space of time labelled work (or leisure). As Aron remarks, it is the intention, not the activity itself, which determines whether it is to be classified as work or leisure.[6]

WORK TIME AND LEISURE TIME

There is a tendency for the length of the working week to decline in most industries, and the 40-hour (or less) *official* working week is rapidly becoming the general standard. But overtime working has been increasing. Although normal hours of work per week fell between 1959 and 1969 by 4 hours to 40·4, the actual hours worked fell by only 2 hours to 44·6.[7] However, earlier retirement (sometimes because of redundancy) and a longer expectation of life are combining to give more time without work to many people. Technical developments in some industries are changing the distribution of, as well as shortening the traditional hours of work, involving four- or even three-day working weeks for some. But over the labour force as a whole the early realization of a drastic reduction in the working week seems unlikely. This is because service occupations account for an increasing proportion of the working population and in these occupations—unlike those in manufacturing industry—there is no tendency for the working week to diminish.[8]

Unless one uses a purely residual definition of leisure as non-working time, there is no necessary connection between hours of work and hours of leisure. Few studies have been made of the duration of leisure, no doubt partly because of the difficulty of defining leisure time. A survey of four occupational groups showed that youth employment and child care employees reported having 33–34 average weekly hours of leisure, and bank and manual workers 42–43.[9] The same survey showed that about three-

[6] R. Aron, *Progress and Disillusion* (Pall Mall Press, 1968), p. 104.

[7] *Department of Employment Gazette*, March 1971, p. 318.

[8] R. Carter, 'The Myth of Increasing Non-work *vs.* Work Activity', *Social Problems*, Summer 1970; see also G. H. Moore and J. N. Hedges, 'Trends in Labor and Leisure', *Monthly Labor Review*, February 1971.

[9] S. R. Parker, *The Future of Work and Leisure* (MacGibbon and Kee, 1971), p. 82.

quarters of certain groups of employees defined leisure as 'only the time you feel free to do whatever you like', and the rest agreed with one of two residual definitions. Although clearly it is unrealistic to expect statistics of leisure to approach the precision of statistics of working weeks, there is scope for improving our knowledge of the amount of time people believe they have as leisure, for example, by mounting an enquiry similar to that carried out by the 13-nation participants in the Multinational Time Budget project.[10] Such an enquiry would need to recognize that leisure can occur at the end of the working day, at the weekend, at the end of the year (holidays), at the end of working life (retirement), and possibly at other times.

VARIABLES AFFECTING THE RELATIONSHIP

The ways in which work and leisure are interrelated are partly a matter of the personality characteristics of the individuals concerned, partly a result of cultural or sub-cultural patterns which influence general behaviour norms, and partly a function of the occupation that an individual follows. Personality is of more central concern to psychologists; the cultural influences, although matters of interest to sociologists, would take us outside the scope of this book; but the sub-cultural influences of occupational experiences *are* relevant.

Data are available on the relation between work and leisure characteristic of a wide variety of occupational groups. Dealing first with the manual group, the decreased physical strain of work has brought about a change in the function of leisure for some manual workers. Thus it has been observed that the jobs of steel workers have now become so relatively lacking in strain that the worker leaves the plant with a good deal of energy to spare, which carries him readily through his leisure hours.[11] However, with industries like mining and farming leisure tends to have a very traditional quality. Tunstall's study of distant-water fishermen showed that leisure during the time they are ashore fulfils the functions of status seeking and of 'explosive compensation' for physically damaging work.[12]

Something of this reaction to work can be seen in the leisure activities of some non-manual workers. Friedmann quotes a study of the leisure occupations of employees at the Postal Cheque

[10] A. Szalai, in R. L. Merritt and S. Rokkan (eds.), *Comparing Nations* (New Haven: Yale University Press, 1966).

[11] D. Riesman, 'Some Observations on Changes in Leisure Attitudes', *Antioch Review*, No. 4, 1952.

[12] J. Tunstall, *The Fishermen* (MacGibbon and Kee, 1962), p. 137.

Centre in Paris, whose jobs are completely routine: on leaving the office these clerks are either much more active or withdraw into themselves in a sort of apathy.[13] But a different pattern of work and leisure is shown by those non-manual employees whose work demands more involvement and responsibility. From their survey, Heckscher and DeGrazia report that the way of life of the American business executive permits no clear-cut distinction between work and leisure.[14] To counteract the encroachment of work on leisure time, the executive's work is penetrated by qualities that we would normally associate with leisure.

The penetration of the businessman's work into the rest of his life is a function of the demands of the work itself rather than of the culture, and Vogel shows the close similarity of the Japanese businessman's life to that of the American.[15] He also notes that, like successful businessmen, doctors rarely make a sharp separation between work and leisure, partly because to some extent working hours are determined by the arrival of patients. It is the salaried man who makes the sharpest distinction between working time and free time. In contrast to the businessman who mixes business and leisure, and to the doctor whose leisure is determined by the absence of patients, the salaried man generally has set hours so that he can plan certain hours of the day and certain days of the week for himself and his family.

Some French sociologists have also done empirical work on the relation between work and leisure. In the preface to a study of pigeon cultivation among miners, Friedmann pointed out that leisure does more than merely offer a compensation for the technique of work.[16] It brings professional compensations for work with a limited horizon, emotional compensations for the crudity of social relations in mass society, and social compensations through the success which this leisure-time activity can provide. After quoting this study, Dumazedier and Latouche note that, far from being a compensation, leisure is more often only an extension of occupational life.

On the other hand, it is possible for the occupational role to provide opportunities for leisure which extend into working time. In a study of British shipyard workers, Brown and his colleagues

[13] G. Friedmann, 'Leisure and Technological Civilization', *International Social Science Journal*, No. 4, 1960.

[14] A. Heckscher and S. DeGrazia, 'Executive Leisure', *Harvard Business Review*, July 1959.

[15] E. F. Vogel, *Japan's New Middle Class* (Berkeley: University of California Press, 1963), p. 21.

[16] Quoted by J. Dumazedier and N. Latouche, 'Work and Leisure in French Sociology', *Industrial Relations*, February 1962.

noted that leisure activities such as exchanging stories and playing cards are an integral part of the work context.[17] They are the cement of social relationships in work and the fabric of the occupational culture. Clearly, the opportunities for leisure-like behaviour in the work situation vary according to such factors as orientation to work, style of supervision, and the extent to which the work demands full and constant attention. There are signs that occupational sociology is beginning to recognize the subtle inter-action of work and leisure.

TOWARDS A THEORY OF WORK AND LEISURE

There are broadly two schools of thought about the relation of spheres of life in urban-industrial society. The first—who may be called segmentalists—hold that society is continuously sub-divided into areas of activity and interest, with each social segment lived out more or less independently of the rest.[18] According to this view, work is separated from leisure, production from con-sumption, workplace from residence, education from religion, politics from recreation.[19] The second school—the 'holists'—maintain that society is now moving towards a fusion of work and leisure. Work, they claim, is now becoming more like play, and play more like work. Attitudes and practices developed in one sphere of life can spill over into another—killing time at work can become killing time in leisure, apathy in the workplace can become apathy in politics, alienation from one, alienation from the other.

The 'fusion' versus 'polarity' hypotheses can be tested against developments in work content, organization and environment. Wilensky cites as evidence of work-leisure fusion the long coffee break among white-collar girls, the lunch 'hour' among top business and professional people, card games among night shift employees; and, off work, the do-it-yourself movement, spare-time jobs, 'customers' golf' for sales executives, and commuter-train conferences for account executives.[20] Also, many devices are being invented for creating spaces of free time during the working day and at intervals through the career. The study of shipyard workers quoted above shows how leisure can penetrate work time

[17] R. Brown et al., 'Leisure in Work', in M. A. Smith et al. (eds.), Society and Leisure in Britain (forthcoming).

[18] R. Dubin, 'Industrial Workers' Worlds', Social Problems, January 1956.

[19] H. Wilensky, 'Work, Careers and Social Integration', International Social Science Journal, No. 4, 1960.

[20] H. Wilensky, 'Mass Society and Mass Culture', American Sociological Review, April 1964.

for at least some kinds of employees, and Dumazedier notes that 'the work group, whether in an enterprise or a company committee, is more and more taking the form of a leisure organization'.[21] In America sabbatical years (or at least 'sabbatical quarters') are no longer exclusive to academic employees, though this practice has not yet spread to Britain.

There are others, however, who take a different view of what is happening to work and leisure. Dismissing evidence of fusion such as that cited above as peripheral to the main structure of modern industry, they seek to show that work has become more concentratedly and actively work. Work may be less arduous physically than it used to be, they say, but its present standards of efficiency require one to key oneself to a higher pitch of nervous and mental effort.[22] The theme of alienation from work is relevant here, since it implies that work as a sphere of human experience is estranged from other spheres such as leisure. Under conditions of present society, it is said, the 'break in consciousness' between work and socialized play, begun during the Industrial Revolution, has been completed.[23]

The evidence is conflicting and the theories built on selections of it are not easily reconcilable. Perhaps the whole fusion versus polarity argument has been carried on at the too general level of society when it should have been applied to the subcultural level of occupations and work milieux. In order to find out more about the work-leisure relationship at this level, Parker carried out a survey among employees in banking, youth employment and child care.[24] These groups are at broadly the same class-status level, but differ substantially in the kind of work they do.

The survey sought to gain information on the relative importance that individuals in certain occupations give to work and leisure spheres in their life pattern. The following patterns emerged: (1) The bank employees characteristically enjoy leisure because it is completely different from work, do not have much of their free time taken up by things connected with their work, and have their central life interest in the family sphere, with leisure second, and (2) the child care and youth employment people characteristically enjoy leisure because it is satisfying in a different way from work,

[21] Dumazedier, *op. cit.*, 1967, p. 78.

[22] C. Greenberg, 'Work and Leisure under Industrialism', in E. Larrabee and R. Meyersohn (eds.), *Mass Leisure* (Glencoe: Free Press, 1958).

[23] This line of argument is developed by A. W. Green, *Recreation, Leisure and Politics* (New York: McGraw-Hill, 1964), pp. 171–2, who does not appear to subscribe to it himself.

[24] Parker, *op. cit.*, Chapter 7.

have a lot of their free time taken up by things connected with their work, and more often have their central life interest in work.

From these survey results, interpreted in the light of previous research on other occupational groups, it appears that there may be three typical ways in which people tend to relate their work to their leisure:

(1) The *extension* pattern consists of having leisure activities that are often similar in content to one's working activities, making no sharp distinction between what is considered work and what is considered leisure, and having one's central life interest in work rather than in family or leisure spheres. This pattern seems to be associated with certain work factors: a high degree of autonomy in the work situation, use of most abilities in the work, high—or, in Etzioni's terms, 'moral'—involvement in the work, and intrinsic satisfaction derived from it. People who exhibit this pattern are likely to have rather little time for activities that they define as leisure, which functions for them mainly as development of personality, and they are probably well-educated. Typical occupations that seem to be associated with this pattern are those of successful businessmen, doctors, teachers, some skilled manual workers, and social workers, especially the kind who live and work on the same premises.

(2) The *neutrality* pattern consists of having leisure activities that are somewhat different from work, making a distinction between work and leisure, and having one's central life interest in family or leisure rather than in the work sphere. The work factors associated with this pattern are: medium to low degree of autonomy in the work situation, use of only some abilities in the work, indifferent or 'calculative' involvement in the work, and satisfaction found in extrinsic work factors such as pay or conditions. In the non-work sphere these individuals are likely to have fairly long hours of leisure, which functions for them chiefly as relaxation, and they have an average level of education. Typical occupations associated with this pattern are those of clerical workers, semi-skilled manual workers, and minor professionals other than social workers.

(3) With the *opposition* pattern leisure activities are definitely unlike work, there is a sharp demarcation between work and leisure, and central life interest is in the non-work sphere. The associated work factors are: low degree of autonomy in the work situation, use of only a narrow range of abilities, hostile or 'alienative' attitude towards work, and satisfaction (if any) found in extrinsic work factors. In the non-work sphere the hours of leisure are likely to be long (though perhaps less regular than with the neutrality pattern), the chief function of leisure is recuperation

from work, and the level of education is generally low. Although this pattern is to some extent exhibited by routine clerical workers, it seems more typical of unskilled manual workers, and those in occupations such as mining and distant-water fishing.

Considerably more research needs to be done to test the validity of these provisional findings and generally to discover more about patterns of work and leisure and types of relation between these two spheres. A knowledge of the ways in which work and leisure are interrelated helps us to understand that the problems of leisure are not likely to be successfully tackled without some consideration of the quality and meaning of working life.

Industrial Sociology at the Crossroads

THIS book has reviewed the major issues, modes of analysis and empirical findings of a field of enquiry that has come to be known as 'industrial sociology'. The content of industrial sociology continues to excite widespread interest, concerning as it does the individual in the world of work, the creation and manipulation of enormous resources through organized effort, and the very institutional fabric of a modern industrialized society itself. The focus upon respectively the individual, the organization and the social system, is reflected in our threefold ordering of the previous chapters. Their content has demonstrated the wide sweep of industrial sociology as well as its obvious practical relevance in a society heavily dependent upon complex organization.

Industrial sociology today is characterized by an extensive subject-matter and by a close interdependence between sociological considerations and those raised by a range of other disciplines such as economics, psychology and production engineering. Interest in the field is prompted by a mixture of motivations including the academic, the idealistic and the commercial. It is not surprising, then, that there are considerable and continuing difficulties in reaching agreement on an appropriate definition, direction and method of development for industrial sociology. Broadly speaking, difficulties arise at two levels. The first involves problems of procedure which industrial sociology shares in large measure with other areas of sociology, and with the social sciences in general. The second level involves problems of identification peculiar to industrial sociology in that they concern the definition of its boundaries and the very basis upon which it survives as a discrete area of study. An appreciation of these disputed issues should assist the student to decide upon his own orientation towards the subject.

Problems of procedure

One long-standing basis of disagreement in industrial sociology is associated with a clash of values between two groups who are both concerned to assist in the solution of what each would regard as pressing problems in the modern industrial world. Each group is in this sense oriented towards serving the needs of a particular client. In the first case the client is the manager and administrator, whose needs are seen to include the improvement of organizational performance, the maintenance of an ordered structure of relationships, and the successful implementation of technological and organizational change. Many social scientists in the United States and a growing number in Western Europe pursue this approach under the general heading of 'action research'.[1] As we have seen in Chapter 8, the major precedent for action research was established by the Hawthorne experiments.

While 'action researchers' exhibit an interest in employee motivation largely from the viewpoint of its bearing on work performance and innovation, the opposing group takes as its point of reference—as its adopted client—the employee himself. Thus there are industrial sociologists who regard the problem of alienation as their main point of departure. They are concerned with studying possibilities for greater self-fulfilment at work rather than those for higher employee performance as defined by management. They are interested in alternative modes of relationships in organizations rather than in improving the operation of existing structures, and they regard industrial change as a means for attaining objectives such as these rather than as a problem of persuading men at work to accept the unpalatable consequences of new managerial policies. While there may be some practical possibilities for reconciling the requirements of these conflicting value systems in the design and operation of organizations, the problem of value conflicts will continue to concern every sociologist whose work has any influence on the conditions within which other people's lives are pursued.

Research strategy provides a second major source of disagreement between industrial sociologists at a 'procedural' level. First, there are those who argue that the major dimensions of the subject can only be ascertained through an extensive comparison across a large number of different cases, employing the sophisticated

---

[1] 'Action Research' is research designed to promote a planned change of selected variables within an on-going system of organized relationships. It should not be confused with the 'social action frame of reference' referred to elsewhere in this book. For a detailed discussion and review of studies see P. A. Clark, *Action Research and Organizational Change* (Harper & Row, 1972).

techniques of measurement and statistical analysis now available. They would argue that the nature of basic parameters such as orientation to work, technology or organizational structure, can only be identified through this approach and that this is equally the case with the further step of establishing the nature of relationships between such parameters. In contrast, there are industrial sociologists, many of them from the 'action research' school, who would insist upon the value of approaching each research situation as a unique constellation of variables. They argue that sociological analysis is refined most effectively through matching the insight obtained from available concepts against the social processes obtaining within a unique situation and against the meanings of that situation to the participants. Important aspects of these processes and meanings may defy quantification. This type of industrial sociologist would stress the limitations attending broad comparative research in that it is forced to rely upon constructs such as 'attitude', 'role' or 'structure', which oversimplify the complexities of empirical data and may impose upon human action a misplaced concreteness and uniformity within the constraints of over-general categories. He would argue instead, with Glaser and Strauss, for a sensitized awareness towards empirical situations, which themselves should provide the main challenge to a sociologist's capacity to offer adequate concepts and schemes of explanation. He would also find support from Argyris' review of the ways in which methods of 'rigorous', primarily quantitative, research can provide distorted results through various types of defensive reaction on the part of respondents.[2]

We have mentioned two sources of contention among industrial sociologists today, which are sufficiently important in their effect to prevent discourse between the various schools of thought from rising much above the level of nodding acquaintance. However, neither of these questions are ones which lead to differentiation and dissension uniquely among industrial sociologists—they are questions which indeed confront most branches of social science today. Furthermore, while such issues do pose important choices for the future direction of the subject, they do not call into doubt the underlying concept of industrial sociology itself by challenging the boundaries that have been drawn around it and upon which its *identification* as a discrete area of enquiry depends. These boundaries have, in fact, been challenged in a way that questions the utility of a study of industry as a separate area of sociological

[2] B. G. Glaser and A. L. Strauss, *The Discovery of Grounded Theory* (Weidenfeld & Nicolson, 1968); C. Argyris, 'Some Unintended Consequences of Rigorous Research', *Psychological Bulletin*, 70, 1968, pp. 185–97.

enquiry; they have equally been challenged in a way that disputes the utility of restricting one's study of industrial behaviour, particularly within organizations, to a purely sociological frame of analysis. These criticisms of the contemporary definition of industrial sociology deserve serious consideration from anyone who is specializing in the area, because they serve to remind him of the limitations which he as a specialist is in danger of imposing upon the interpretation of his subject matter.

Problems of identification

The first criticism against the contemporary definitions of industrial sociology, discussed in Chapter 1, is that these represent an academic demarcation between industrial and non-industrial sociology which has led to a division of interest that is empirically artificial. It may be that in a formal sense the structures and technologies of industry are discrete from those of other social institutions, but these of themselves are not of sociological significance. Rather, it is the purposes which led to the establishment of such structures, the ends to which they are adapted, the meaning they have for those who participate in them and the consequences they have both for those participants and for other groups affected by their operations, which are the sociologically interesting features. In other words, structures and technologies only assume sociological significance through the actors in the situations where the structures and technologies operate. But these actors do not normally lead lives and have hopes, fears and values which are either limited to industry and its operation or are compartmentalized between the spheres of work and non-work.

In this respect, then, the division between industrial sociology and sociology in general is difficult to justify. It is apparent from research on orientations to work, and particularly on the nexus between work and leisure, that the meaning of work to an individual has to be appreciated in terms of his perspective on his life as a whole, not just his life as a member of an industrial organization. For the same reason, a person's orientation towards leisure time cannot be fully understood without reference to his role in the sphere of work. It is in this sense that work and leisure only have a full sociological meaning in relation to each other. Much the same point has been made recently in a discussion of industrial sabotage, namely that the motives for sabotage and its meaning to the saboteurs in industry are matched by similar motives and meanings outside industry where the same action is given the different term of vandalism. The significance of such acts both within industry and outside it to those perpetrating them may be identical and may derive from a location in the same kind of social situation—indeed the same man may well be responsible.[3] A further illustration of the general point at issue comes from workers' reactions to attributes of their jobs. Two American studies found that workers who came from small town and rural backgrounds showed a positive response in terms of satisfaction to job attributes which allowed for greater variety, responsibility and the like, while workers in large urban settings responded negatively to the same job attributes. In both cases the only plausible explanation for such results lies in reference to the different systems of social values held by the two groups of workers.[4] Any perspective which is limited to the industrial context would fail to account for findings such as these.

To pursue this argument is to go a good deal further than merely saying that general insights from sociology need to be applied to industry as a particular area of study, if all this means is that use is made of general sociological concepts and modes of analysis. While these are essential, an objection can be made against industrial sociology as such to the effect that it misleadingly implies a segregation of thought and action between the industrial and other social contexts. For this reason some critics would argue that the aims of industrial sociology should be those of sociology in general, and a view is held, for example, that there is a fundamental incompatibility between the perspectives which should be adopted by sociologists focusing upon industry and those which have up to now been adopted in practice by many investigators.[5] In this view, a sociologist may perhaps conveniently be called an 'industrial sociologist' to denote the empirical area in which his enquiries will be concentrated. However, his analytical frame of reference would not be confined to the sphere of industry or work, while the direction of his enquiries would move towards the elucidation of issues which contribute to the central themes of sociology itself. Examples of such issues would be the relationship between economic position and ideology, the social bases for conflict and consensus, mechanisms of social control, social consequences of bureaucratic organization, and the question of alienation.

[3] L. Taylor and P. Walton, 'Industrial Sabotage: Motives and Meanings', in S. Cohen (ed.), *Images of Deviance* (Penguin, 1971), pp. 219-45.
[4] A. N. Turner and P. R. Lawrence, *Industrial Jobs and the Worker* (Boston: Harvard Business School, 1965); C. L. Hulin and M. R. Blood, 'Job Enlargement, Individual differences and Worker Responses', *Psychological Bulletin*, 69, 1968, pp. 41-55.
[5] Cf. M. Albrow, 'The Study of Organizations—Objectivity or Bias?', in J. Gould (ed.), *Penguin Social Sciences Survey*, 1968, pp. 146-67.

Rex, a few years ago, listed a number of questions which were then coming to engage the attention of sociologists and which necessarily made heavy reference to the sphere of industry—'is it the case that advanced capitalist societies have solved their major problems of economic and political stability? Is it the case that the working-class has now been successfully "incorporated" into the value-system . . .? Is there a common level of mobility which is achieved by all societies at a certain level of industrial advancement? In what ways are the motivations of owners, managers and workers tied into the organization of the modern corporation?'[6] Other subjects of enquiry which would fall within the scope of this revised definition of industrial sociology include the question of how a person's quality of life is associated with his experience at work, and the extent to which the forms of structured relationships found in industrial organizations reflect the pressures of economic and technological exigencies rather than being the manifestation of cultural values and ideological preferences. Many of these examples echo the concerns of Marx and Weber and indeed this is the charter for a sociology of industry which they and other pioneers of sociology set out. There are many who would claim that Marx and Weber with their concern to arrive at an understanding of economic and social relationships in general have provided what are still the most insightful analyses of the industrial sphere as a particular case. Clearly, in this objection to the present definition of industrial sociology, can be seen a signpost beckoning industrial sociologists towards one of the main routes which they might travel in the future.

The other major challenge to the contemporary definition of industrial sociology has been well expressed in an important paper by Landsberger. Referring primarily to the American context, he concludes that since the mid-1950s there has been 'what is, in effect, a complete reconceptualization—in a sense, a downgrading —of industrial sociology and industrial social psychology. These fields are now but a part of a much more comprehensive study of all kinds of organizations. There is widespread recognition that whatever characteristics may be especially pronounced in organizations in the economic sector of society, these characteristics are best highlighted through deliberate contrast with organizations in other sectors of society. The scientific analysis of—and the practitioner's need to understand—the nature of managerial authority in industry, for example, is facilitated by comparing it with authority in armies, public administration generally and welfare

[6] J. Rex, 'Which Path for Sociology?', New Society, October 6, 1966, p. 529.

agencies and prisons specifically, voluntary associations, schools, hospitals, research laboratories, and trade unions.'[7]

Landsberger here is pointing to the limitations of studying industrial phenomena in isolation, but the brunt of his thesis is that a great deal is lost by confining one's analysis of any empirically defined area through applying the perspectives of only one discipline such as sociology. Rather, much is to be gained, at least for some purposes, by bringing all the resources of social science to bear upon a particular issue, and by comparing and contrasting in an orderly fashion the insights of the different disciplines even if they cannot as yet be welded together within the confines of a single, over-arching theory. This is to say, 'stated positively, our thesis is that all of behavioral science—and the non-behavioral social sciences too—are applicable to industry, work and organizations. The student would do best to take a single problem—say, unemployment or professionalization, or perhaps selection—to see how the different social sciences have approached its analysis. This is likely to be more enlightening and stimulating than taking a single one of the social sciences . . . and examining all the possible and very diverse problems relevant to it'.[8] Landsberger is therefore not only contending that the concept of *industrial* sociology is too restrictive because it inhibits valuable comparison between the industrial and other spheres of social life, but he is also arguing that it is of value to combine the contributions of all the social sciences in one's analysis and that this means that attention has to be focused on specific issues and problems in order to be at all manageable.

Landsberger mentioned that, in the United States at least, industrial sociology had now to a large extent become absorbed into a comprehensive study of all kinds of organizations. An increasing body of work in Britain has also come to adopt this strategy, which passes under the heading of organizational behaviour. There is a concentration on studying the structure and functioning of organizations (including non-industrial ones) and on the orientations and behaviours of groups and individuals within organizations. This sub-discipline makes use of concepts drawn from management theorists, students of bureaucracy, social psychologists, industrial economists and students of technology, in addition to the contributions of industrial sociologists. Sociology is therefore only one contributory discipline to the development of organizational behaviour.

[7] H. A. Landsberger, 'The Behavioral Sciences in Industry', *Industrial Relations*, October 7, 1967, pp. 1–19.
[8] *Op. cit.*, p. 1.

Organizational behaviour seeks to utilize the contributions of all the social sciences in seeking to reach an understanding of attitudes, action and structured relationships. Thus within organizational behaviour one finds 'organizational psychologists' pursuing investigations which are beginning to suggest links between previous work on technology, organization structure and community value systems as points of reference for the explanation of behaviour.[9] Similarly, connections are developing between the work of economists and sociologists through studies of 'managerial capitalism', while the focus on organizational analysis has encouraged a fruitful exchange of concepts and propositions between students of business, of hospitals and public organizations, and of trade unions.[10]

It might appear, nevertheless, that this multi-disciplinary effort, focusing as it does upon organization, is being directed to an empirically restricted area. Its advocates would argue that in advanced societies at least, formal organization permeates social life to such an extent that it can be considered as a legitimate centre-point of analysis. Within this field many investigators have espoused the concept of open systems, partly to emphasize the interdependence between organization and social activity in general, and partly because they find that it has the advantage of drawing attention to the relations between action and context at any level of analysis. In this respect an open systems approach serves to highlight the continuum of explanation running from the level of individual personality dynamics through to the function of whole societies in their own inter-societal context. One could regard the three constituent parts of this book as having been concerned with a section of this continuum— ranging from the level of person-role interaction, through the role-organization level, to the institution-social system level. Although some 'system theorists' have employed sociologically naïve organic analogies, an open systems perspective as such does not rely upon any assumption that social organizations have a life of their own, or that they are anything other than the product of human decision and action.

Many sociologists, as we have seen in Chapter 7, have expressed dissatisfaction with the type of organizational analysis which has tended to predominate in recent years. Partly because of its

---

[9] E.g., Hulin and Blood, *op. cit.*; see also R. P. Quinn and R. L. Kahn, 'Organizational Psychology', in *Annual Review of Psychology*, 18, 1967, pp. 437–66.
[10] E.g., R. M. Cyert and J. G. March, *A Behavioral Theory of the Firm* (Englewood Cliffs, N.J.: Prentice-Hall, 1963); J. G. March (ed.), *Handbook of Organizations* (Chicago: Rand McNally, 1965).

historical links with administrative theory and the continuing association of many students with the practical problems of management, much organizational analysis has relied very heavily upon the use of concepts such as equilibrium, order, and structure, with their implication that a stable and cohesive system of effort directed towards a commonly accepted objective could be taken as the normal point of reference for analysis. Associated with this way of thinking has been a sociologically unsatisfactory tendency towards misplaced concreteness and reification in the use of concepts such as role and organization; indeed, it is not unusual in this literature to find organizations being accorded the personal qualities of holding objectives and of pursuing behaviour. In addition, the types of theory which have emerged from the study of organizational behaviour are notable for adopting a deterministic emphasis which not only detracts from the undoubted opportunities for exercising choice in the design of organizational arrangements but, equally important, which fails to recognize that people do in very important ways actually exercise choice in pursuing their personal and collective strategies within organizational contexts.[11] However, these problems are coming to be recognized by a new generation of sociologists interested in organizational activities and they should not of themselves lead one to dismiss the case which Landsberger has advanced for a move away from traditional definitions of industrial sociology, and which organizational behaviour in principle satisfies as a strategy of investigation.

Recent formulations of industrial relations as an area of study provide a further alternative framework within which to develop much of the subject-matter of industrial sociology as it is now defined. Largely under the influence of Dunlop's theory of 'industrial relations systems', many students of industrial relations are today moving beyond a purely descriptive formal and institutional approach towards a treatment of the work organization as an open social system in which the structure of formal procedure and its connections with external institutions is but one of a number of relevant and related aspects. This new methodology of industrial relations, like that of organizational behaviour, allows the use of theoretical tools from a number of specialist disciplines of which sociology is one. 'Thus, it permits the use of a sociological concept, such as status, a psychological concept, such as personality, and economic factors, such as the product and factor markets. As these theoretical tools are applied within

---

[11] J. Child, 'Organizational Structure, Environment and Performance—The Role of Strategic Choice', *Sociology*, January 1972.

the area of industrial relations they will probably take on similarities which distinguish them from those used in the fields in which they originated.'[12]

Those who wish to return industrial sociology to the mainstream of sociological development will view this prospect of conceptual particularism with alarm. Those who sympathize with Landsberger's view will, on the other hand, claim that sociology itself can have little relevance if it is not concerned with human thought and action, and that this thought and action cannot be neatly compartmentalized into the boxes supplied by traditionally defined academic disciplines. Some would, perhaps, go further and maintain that the pursuit of research within frameworks such as organizational behaviour and industrial relations only represent convenient stages on the way to attaining a mature social science. The criterion is whether new bounded areas of enquiry such as these enhance our understanding through the development of theory that integrates relevant propositions more effectively than that so far available.

In conclusion, we would reaffirm that the subject matter of this book is of central significance for an understanding of human endeavours within our contemporary industrial societies. The prime requirement for the sociologist is never to lose sight of the fact that every institution, organization and technology is a product of human decision and action and that it has no existence in its own right apart from these. Once this perspective is accepted as the guideline for investigation, then a diversity of analytical strategies is likely to prove more of a strength than a weakness. There is certainly no reason to cling to a traditional definition of industrial sociology for its own sake. Many have become dissatisfied with the path of development which industrial sociologists have so far pursued, and would urge them, standing at the crossroads, to consider changing direction in one or other of the ways we have described.

[12] J. T. Dunlop, *Industrial Relations Systems* (New York: Holt, 1958); A. N. J. Blain and J. Gennard, 'Industrial Relations Theory—A Critical Review', *British Journal of Industrial Relations*, November 1970, pp. 389–407.

Selected Further Reading

(Place of publications below and in footnotes is London unless otherwise stated)

PART I

There are no British textbooks covering substantially the whole area of industrial sociology as defined widely in this book. J. E. T. Eldridge, *Sociology and Industrial Life*, Michael Joseph, 1971, relates recent empirical investigations to classic sociological theory and contemporary theoretical perspectives. The chapter by D. H. J. Morgan and R. Ward, 'Work, Industry and Organizations', in P. Worsley, *Introducing Sociology*, Penguin, 1970 is a similar review, with more comparative emphasis. A. Fox, *A Sociology of Work in Industry*, Collier-Macmillan, 1971 is a closely reasoned account of much of the field, especially industrial relations. A collection of readings with a wide coverage is T. Burns (ed.), *Industrial Man*, Penguin, 1969. Two outstanding American textbooks are D. C. Miller and W. H. Form, *Industrial Sociology*, New York: Harper and Row, 1964, and E. V. Schneider, *Industrial Sociology*, New York: McGraw-Hill, 2nd edn., 1969.

Probably the best concise theoretical work on the economic sub-system is N. J. Smelser, *The Sociology of Economic Life*, Englewood Cliffs: Prentice-Hall, 1963. P. W. Musgrave, *The Economic Structure*, Longman, 1969 is a good factual summary. P. S. Florence, *Economics and Sociology of Industry*, Watts, 2nd edn., 1969 contains a useful discussion of trends in the British economy. G. C. Allen, *The Structure of Industry in Britain*, Longman, 1970 is a reference work. Important and stimulating works discussing the general development of the economic and industrial system are J. K. Galbraith, *The New Industrial State*, Penguin, 1969 and E. J. Mishan, *The Costs of Economic Growth*, Penguin, 1969.

Several chapters on aspects of industry and education are in A. H. Halsey *et al.* (eds.), *Education, Economy and Society*, Glencoe: Free Press, 1961. The transition from school to work is dealt with in N. B. Keene, *The Employment of Young Workers*, Batsford, 1969 and E. J. Maizels, *Adolescent Needs and the Transition from School to Work*, Athlone Press, 1970. S. Cotgrove, *Technical Education and Social Change*, Allen & Unwin, 1958 gives a critical account of the development of technical education, and G. Williams, *Recruitment to Skilled Trades*, Routledge, 1957 does the same for apprenticeship.

Work and family variables are dealt with in R. O. Blood and D. M. Wolfe, *Husbands and Wives*, Glencoe: Free Press, 1960 and D. C. McKinley, *Social Class and Family Life*, Glencoe: Free Press, 1964. Two British books which deal in part with this subject are E. Bott, *Family and Social Network*, Tavistock, 1957 and R. Rapoport *et al.*, *Leisure and the Family Life Cycle*, Routledge, 1975. The subject of married women working is discussed in M. P. Fogarty, *Sex, Career and Family*, Allen & Unwin, 1971 and a more factual account is A. Hunt, *A Survey of Women's Employment*, HMSO, 1968.

Class and status as forms of stratification based on economic position are dealt with in T. B. Bottomore, *Classes in Modern Society*, Allen & Unwin, 1965 and R. Dahrendorf, *Class and Class Conflict in an Industrial Society*, Routledge, 1963 and more specifically in relation to occupational groups in D. Lockwood, *The Blackcoated Worker*, Allen & Unwin, 1958 and K. Prandy, *Professional Employees*, Faber, 1965. The 'embourgeoisement thesis' is discussed in J. H. Goldthorpe *et al.*, *The Affluent Worker in the Class Structure*, Cambridge: University Press, 1969. A good collection of essays is M. M. Tumin (ed.), *Readings Social Stratification*, Englewood Cliffs: Prentice-Hall, 1970.

The theory of industry–community relations is dealt with in W. H. Form and D. C. Miller, *Industry, Labor and Community*, New York: Harper, 1960. Aspects of the industrial influence on politics and the political constraints on industry are discussed respectively in A. Potter, *Organized Groups in British National Politics*, Faber, 1961 and J. W. Grove, *Government and Industry in Britain*, Longmans, 1962. K. W. Wedderburn, *The Worker and the Law*, MacGibbon and Kee, 2nd edn., 1971, is one of the best works in its field.

PART II

Most of the extensive published work on organization theory is American, but two notable British contributions are D. Silverman, *The Theory of Organisations*, Heinemann, 1970 and N. P. Mouzelis, *Organisation and Bureaucracy*, Routledge, 1967. Important texts published in Britain by American writers include P. M. Blau and W. R. Scott, *Formal Organizations*, Routledge, 1963 and C. Perrow, *Organizational Analysis*, Tavistock, 1970. A. Etzioni, *A Comparative Analysis of Complex Organizations*, Glencoe: Free Press, 1961 is a significant theoretical contribution; P. R. Lawrence and J. Lorsch, *Organization and Environment*, Cambridge, Mass.: Harvard University Press, 1967 deals more particularly with the effect of an organization's environment on its internal structure and behaviour, and C. Argyris, *The Applicability of Organizational Sociology*, Cambridge University Press, 1972, deals with the problem of organizational change. Several readers are available in the subject, notably A. Etzioni, *Complex Organiza-*

tions : A Sociological Reader, New York: Holt, Rinehart, 2nd edn., 1969 and J. G. March, *Handbook of Organizations*, Chicago: Rand McNally, 1965.

A good introduction to the development of the Human Relations movement and studies of the work group is still G. Friedmann, *Industrial Society*, Glencoe: Free Press, 1955. The full account of the Hawthorne Experiments is F. J. Roethlisberger and W. J. Dickson, *Management and the Worker*, Cambridge, Mass.: Harvard University Press, 1939, and New York: Wiley, 1964. The views of Elton Mayo are most accessible in *The Social Problems of an Industrial Civilization*, Routledge, 1949. H. A. Landsberger, *Hawthorne Revisited*, Ithaca, N.Y.: Cornell University Press, 1958 provides a balanced account of the Hawthorne studies and of much of the subsequent criticism. The more recent work in this tradition is outlined in E. H. Schein, *Organizational Psychology*, Englewood Cliffs, N. J.: Prentice-Hall, 1965. Studies of working groups are reported in L. R. Sayles, *Behaviour of Industrial Work Groups*, New York: Wiley, 1958, T. Lupton, *On the Shop Floor*, Oxford: Pergamon, 1963, and S. Cunnison, *Wages and Work Allocation*, Tavistock, 1966.

A valuable collection of readings on technology and technical change is C. R. Walker (ed.), *Technology, Industry and Man*, New York: McGraw-Hill, 1968 (1962 edition entitled *Modern Technology and Civilization*); S. Marcson (ed.), *Automation, Alienation and Anomie*, New York: Harper, 1970 is also very useful. J. Woodward, *Industrial Organization : Theory and Practice*, Oxford University Press, 1965 and R. Blauner, *Alienation and Freedom*, Chicago: University Press, 1964 are two leading examples of the 'technological implications' approach which is criticized in J. H. Goldthorpe *et al.*, *The Affluent Worker : Industrial Attitudes and Behaviour*, Cambridge University Press, 1968. The impact of technical change is discussed in general in T. Burns and G. M. Stalker, *The Management of Innovation*, Tavistock, 1960 and A. Touraine *et al.*, *Workers' Attitudes to Technical Change*, Paris: OECD, 1965. P. Sadler, *Social Research on Automation*, SSRC/Heinemann, 1968 is a useful review of the literature on automation. For recent general discussions of social relations in industry, see J. Child (ed.), *Man and Organization*, Allen & Unwin, 1972, and M. Warner (ed.), *The Sociology of the Workplace*, Allen & Unwin, 1973.

Most works on management are concerned with technical issues rather than with a sociological analysis. C. Sofer, *Men in Mid-Career*, Cambridge University Press, 1970, provides a readable and extensive review of studies on managers. T. Burns and G. M. Stalker, *The Management of Innovation*, Tavistock, 1961, is an insightful British study into political processes within management, while M. Dalton, *Men Who Manage*, Wiley, 1959, is an American study based on many years of participant observation.

H. Mintzberg, *The Nature of Managerial Work*, New York: Harper & Row, 1973, is a comprehensive study. M. Z. Brooke and H. L. Remmers, *The Strategy of Multinational Enterprise*, Longman, 1970, reports detailed research on the internal operations of multinational managements. T. Lupton, *Management and the Social Sciences*, Penguin, 2nd edn., 1971, summarizes many relevant studies, while J. Child, *The Business Enterprise in Modern Industrial Society*, Collier-Macmillan, 1969, is a guide to major issues and available literature.

The literature on industrial relations grows rapidly, and in some respects rapidly becomes out of date. Among recent works are two good collections of readings: B. C. Roberts (ed.), *Industrial Relations: Contemporary Problems and Perspectives*, Methuen, 1968 and H. Clegg (ed.), *The System of Industrial Relations in Great Britain*, Oxford: Blackwell, 2nd edn., 1972. N. Robertson and J. L. Thomas, *Trade Unions and Industrial Relations*, Business Books, 1968 is a good general textbook, while J. E. T. Eldridge, *Industrial Disputes: Essays in the Sociology of Industrial Relations*, Routledge, 1968 deals more specifically with industrial conflict. Two different approaches to industrial participation are E. Roberts, *Workers' Control*, Allen & Unwin, 1973, and N. S. Ross, *Constructive Conflict*, Edinburgh: Oliver and Boyd, 1969.

PART III

Most books on the sociology of work and occupations are American. M. L. Taylor, *Occupational Sociology*, New York: Oxford University Press, 1968 covers most aspects of the subject, as does R. H. Hall, *Occupations and the Social Structure*, New York: Prentice-Hall, 1969. A good reader is S. Nosow and W. H. Form (eds.), *Man, Work and Society*, New York: Basic Books, 1962. P. M. Blau and O. D. Duncan, *The American Occupational Structure*, New York: Wiley, 1967 deals chiefly with mobility, and A. Harris, *Labour Mobility in Great Britain 1953–63*, Government Social Survey, 1966 is a factual report.

Two British sources on the subjective experience of work are J. H. Goldthorpe *et al.*, *The Affluent Worker: Industrial Attitudes and Behaviour*, Cambridge University Press, 1968 and H. Beynon and R. M. Blackburn, *Perceptions of Work*, Cambridge University Press, 1972. Other books in this field are chiefly American. On work ideologies there is R. Bendix, *Work and Authority in Industry*, New York: Wiley, 1957; on values and occupational choice, M. Rosenberg *et al.*, *Occupations and Values*, Glencoe: Free Press, 1957; on alienation, R. Blauner, *Alienation and Freedom*, Chicago: University Press, 1964; and on motivation and job satisfaction, F. Herzberg, *Work and the Nature of Man*, Staples Press, 1968.

A recent book devoted wholly to the relationship between work and leisure is S. R. Parker, *The Future of Work and Leisure*, MacGibbon and Kee, 1971. N. Anderson, *Work and Leisure*, Routledge, 1961 brings together a wide variety of research findings and more general observations. J. Dumazedier, *Toward a Society of Leisure*, Collier-Macmillan, 1967 has a chapter on work and leisure.

Index